POLICIES AND RESEARCH
IN IDENTITY MANAGEMENT

IFIP – The International Federation for Information Processing

IFIP was founded in 1960 under the auspices of UNESCO, following the First World Computer Congress held in Paris the previous year. An umbrella organization for societies working in information processing, IFIP's aim is two-fold: to support information processing within its member countries and to encourage technology transfer to developing nations. As its mission statement clearly states,

> *IFIP's mission is to be the leading, truly international, apolitical organization which encourages and assists in the development, exploitation and application of information technology for the benefit of all people.*

IFIP is a non-profitmaking organization, run almost solely by 2500 volunteers. It operates through a number of technical committees, which organize events and publications. IFIP's events range from an international congress to local seminars, but the most important are:

• The IFIP World Computer Congress, held every second year;
• Open conferences;
• Working conferences.

The flagship event is the IFIP World Computer Congress, at which both invited and contributed papers are presented. Contributed papers are rigorously refereed and the rejection rate is high.

As with the Congress, participation in the open conferences is open to all and papers may be invited or submitted. Again, submitted papers are stringently refereed.

The working conferences are structured differently. They are usually run by a working group and attendance is small and by invitation only. Their purpose is to create an atmosphere conducive to innovation and development. Refereeing is less rigorous and papers are subjected to extensive group discussion.

Publications arising from IFIP events vary. The papers presented at the IFIP World Computer Congress and at open conferences are published as conference proceedings, while the results of the working conferences are often published as collections of selected and edited papers.

Any national society whose primary activity is in information may apply to become a full member of IFIP, although full membership is restricted to one society per country. Full members are entitled to vote at the annual General Assembly, National societies preferring a less committed involvement may apply for associate or corresponding membership. Associate members enjoy the same benefits as full members, but without voting rights. Corresponding members are not represented in IFIP bodies. Affiliated membership is open to non-national societies, and individual and honorary membership schemes are also offered.

POLICIES AND RESEARCH
IN IDENTITY MANAGEMENT

First IFIP WG11.6 Working Conference on Policies and Research in Identity Management (IDMAN'07), RSM Erasmus University, Rotterdam, The Netherlands, October 11-12, 2007

Edited by

Elisabeth de Leeuw
Ordina N.V.
The Netherlands

Simone Fischer-Hübner
Karlstad University
Sweden

Jimmy Tseng
RSM Erasmus University
The Netherlands

John Borking
Borking Consultancy
The Netherlands

 Springer

Policies and Research in Identity Management

Edited by Elisabeth de Leeuw, Simone Fischer-Hübner, Jimmy Tseng, and John Borking

p. cm. (IFIP International Federation for Information Processing, a Springer Series in Computer Science)

ISSN: 1571-5736 / 1861-2288 (Internet)
ISBN: 978-1-4419-4609-6
eISBN: 978-0-387-77996-6

Printed on acid-free paper

Printed in the United States of America.

9 8 7 6 5 4 3 2 1

springer.com

Foreword

The world of the 21st century is, more than ever, global and impersonal. Criminal and terrorist threats, both physical and on the Internet, increase by the day. The demand for better methods of identification and access control is growing, not only in companies and organisations but also in the world at large. At the same time, such security measures have to be balanced with means for protecting the privacy of users.

Identity management is put under pressure, due to the growing number of frauds who want to hide their true identity. This challenges the information security research community to focus on interdisciplinary and holistic approaches while retaining the benefits of previous research efforts.

In this context, the IFIP Working Group 11.6 on Identity Management has been founded in August 2006. The intention of the Working Group is to offer a broad forum for the exchange of knowledge and for the tracking and discussion of issues and new developments. In this, we take an interdisciplinary approach. Scientists as well as practitioners, from government and business, who are involved in the field of identity management are welcome to participate.

The IDMAN 2007 Conference on Policies and Research in Identity Management was the very first conference organized by this Working Group. We aim to organize conferences bi-annually.

The IDMAN 2007 Conference has been centered around the theme of National Identity Management or, in other words, identity management in the public sector. National identity management plays a central role, not only in immigration and border control processes but also in identity management and access control processes of many companies and organisations around the world. New employees are asked for a passport when entering a company. Clients of a bank are legally obliged to show a passport when opening a new account. This raises many security and privacy questions.

In anticipation of the conference, a call for papers has been broadcasted. The subsequently submitted papers were in general of high quality. Each paper was reviewed by two or three reviewers and for the paper selection process no concessions have been made to the quality. I was delighted to find that a high level audience attended the conference, appreciated the program and participated actively in discussions.

First, I am grateful to the Rotterdam School of Management, who hosted the conference in an excellent manner and made it a pleasure for everybody, for organizers, speakers and participants alike.

Thanks also the organizers, programme committee, speakers and sponsors and to the authors of the submitted papers.

Special thanks also to the keynote speakers whose contributions made the program appealing: Gus Hosein of the London School of Economics; Fred Carter, representative of the Information and Privacy Commissioner, Ontario, CA.; Dirk van

Rooy of the Directorate General Information Society and Media and Eddy Higgs, University of Essex, UK.

Furthermore, I would like to thank the moderators of and participants in the Expert Panels who presented the audience with a challenging discussion.

Elisabeth de Leeuw

Ordina N.V., The Netherlands
Chair of IFIP WG11.6
IDMAN 2007 Conference General Chair

Organisation

IDMAN'07 was organized by IFIP Working Group 11.6 in cooperation with the Erasmus University of Rotterdam.

Conference General Chair
Elisabeth de Leeuw, Ordina N.V., The Netherlands

Programme Committee Co-Chairs
Simone Fischer-Hübner, Karlstad University, Sweden
Jimmy C. Tseng, RSM Erasmus University, The Netherlands
John Borking, Borking Consultancy, The Netherlands

Local Organising Committee
Marcel van Oosterhout, RSM Erasmus University, The Netherlands
Jimmy C. Tseng, RSM Erasmus University, The Netherlands

International Program Committee
Keith Breckenridge, University of Natal, Durban, South Africa
Hans Hedbom, Karlstad University, Sweden
Ian Hosein, Privacy International and London School of Economics, United Kingdom
Bart Jacobs, University of Nijmegen, The Netherlands
Alfred Kobsa, University of California Irvine, USA
Ronald Leenes, University of Tilburg, The Netherlands
Miriam Lips, Victoria University of Wellington, New Zealand
Marit Hansen, Unabhängiges Landeszentrum für Datenschutz (ICCP), Germany
Pedro Luis Muñoz, Telefonica, Spain
Ruud van Munster, Netherlands Organisation of Applied Research TNO, The Netherlands
Aljosa Pasic, Atos Origin, Spain
Reinhard Posch, Austrian Federal Chancellery, Austria
Andreas Pfitzmann, TU Dresden, Germany
Kai Rannenberg, Frankfurt University, Germany
Stefanos Gritzalis, University of the Aegean, Greece
Leon Strous, De Nederlandsche Bank, The Netherlands
Raymond Veldhuis, University of Twente, the Netherlands

Additional Reviewers
Mike Bergmann, Elke Franz, Herbert Leitold, Leonardo Martucci, Udo Payer, Jan Zibuschka

Table of Contents

Identity and Privacy Protection

Authentication

Analysis of Identification Schemes

Politics and Identity Management

Gus Hosein

The London School of Economics and Political Science

Extended synopsis

The field of identity management has changed dramatically in just a few years. Ten years ago we were huddled in the corner of cocktail parties excitedly discussing and dismissing X.509 certification. Five years ago we were begging for some attention from our governments, industries, and consumer protection institutions. Now, everyone seems to be in agreement that something must be done about identity management.

This is indeed a moment of validation. Identity Management's time has come. If you thought it was going to get easier now that everyone is interested, you are in for a big surprise.

As some companies like Microsoft have learned, as have any number of governments, implementing an identity policy is fraught with problems. In fact, the problem begins well before the implementation stage but rather with the process of developing an identity policy.

In the research from the London School of Economics and Political Science about identity policy schemes around the world, we have been able to identify a number of common threads within many of the political and technological debates. We summarise these as the dynamics of identity policy:

1. There are always political risks.

Even when governments and organisations are sure that they have complete buy-in, it is highly probably that political problems will follow. In the UK, New Zealand, and Australia support for new policies were at first above 80%, but quickly fell.

2. There are uncertain drivers for change.

Proponents of policy change are often unsure of how to sell their changes. They reach too often for convenient arguments rather than well thought out arguments. Evidence can be chosen amongst the many identity policy failures since the rise of terrorism concerns, or ineffectual identity fraud policies in the wake of growing consumer concerns. There is an increasingly common list of drivers for identity policy, many of which have little to do with the actual reasons for introducing policy change.

3. There is a divide between what proponents dream and what is deliverable.

There are far too few feasibility checks on both the goals of policy change and the actual implementations. Politicians and decision-makers get carried away with building vast new infrastructures of registration and processing without considering classical problems of implementation, such as market and network effects, and large-scale management challenges.

Please use the following format when citing this chapter:

Hosein, G., 2008, in IFIP International Federation for Information Processing, Volume 261; *Policies and Research in Identity Management*; Eds. E. de Leeuw, Fischer-Hübner, S., Tseng, J., Borking, J.; (Boston: Springer), pp. 3–4.

4. Choices are easily made but rarely are they effective.

Policy is quickly established, often in a rush to respond to new developments, but rarely with adequate consideration. New technologies are chosen without considering their limitations. It is not that the technologies may fail, but rather their ideal operating conditions are not conducive to the policy choices.

5. After the excitement of deciding upon new policies, costs always creep in.

Costs arise from design decisions, where costs are likely to rise in highly centralised, technology-driven solutions. The moment biometrics enter into the frame, costs are necessarily higher as we have to include registration centres, regular renewal of biometrics, and readers across the entire infrastructure. These are rarely considered within policy processes.

6. The shape of the policy is often dictated by the policy-owner.

Though this may seem quite a deterministic point, we have found that when law enforcement-oriented agencies are responsible for devising identity policies they develop one that reflects their interest in law enforcement. These lead to centralised systems that uniquely identify all individuals. But when administrative agencies develop identity policies they tend to create more flexible and possibly distributed schemes.

7. Identity policies usually cater for civil liberties and privacy at too late a stage.

Increasingly identity policies are driven by technological change and opportunities, or political debates that respond to events. These drivers often lead to schemes that then need to gain public acceptance, and it is usually at that point that decision-makers and technologists speak of civil liberties and privacy. Companies' and governments' projects have failed when they fell into this chain of events.

To conclude, identity policy's time has come, but at the same time we believe that this is the opportunity to finally raise the level of the debate. Now that we no longer have to expend considerable resources in convincing people in the need for change, we may now finally start speaking about the true nature of problems and find evolved methods of deliberation and decision-making.

To date, the decision-making processes, whether the political processes within governments or the product-design discussions in companies, have not proven to be the best way to come up with design specifications for identity policy. They tend to be driven by ideals rather than consultation. These ideals may be of how to perfectly order society or how to perfectly harness new technological developments. When we are dealing with policies that affect large populations who may not share these ideals or face conditions that do not adhere to design requirements we are likely to see even further policy failures.

Identity management researchers must therefore begin considering the near-inevitable problem of politics. Only then we may better understand how identity works outside of both the laboratories and the corridors of power.

Insecure Flight: Broken Boarding Passes and Ineffective Terrorist Watch Lists

Christopher Soghoian

Indiana University Bloomington, School of Informatics
Indiana, USA
csoghoian@gmail.com

Abstract. In this paper, we discuss a number of existing problems with the airport transportation security system in the United States. We discuss two separate, yet equally important issues: The ease with which a passenger can fly without any identification documents at all and the ease with which print-at-home boarding passes can be modified, tampered with, and faked. The significance of these vulnerabilities becomes clear when viewed in light of the US government's insistence on maintaining passenger watch lists, whose contents are secret and effectiveness depend upon the government being able to verify the identity of each flying passenger. We then introduce a method of determining if any particular name is on the no fly list, without ever having to step foot into an airport. We introduce a physical denial of service attack against the Transportation Security Administration (TSA) checkpoints at airports, distributed via an Internet virus. Finally, we propose technical solutions to the user modifiable boarding pass problem, which also neutralize the physical denial of service attack. The solutions have the added benefit of meshing with TSA's publicly stated wish to assume responsibility for verifying passengers names against the watch lists, as well as enabling them to collect and store real time data on passengers as they pass through checkpoints, something they are currently not able to do.

1 Introduction

Since September 11 2001, the US government has placed tens of thousands of American travelers on watch lists as part of a massive security initiative that affects all of the nearly seven hundred million passengers who fly within the United States annually [17]. The Transportation Security Administration (TSA) supplies airlines with two watch lists, against which their staff must compare each passenger who flies. The watch lists contain names of people barred from boarding a commercial aircraft unless they are cleared by law enforcement officers (the "no fly" list) and those who are given greater security attention (the "selectee" list) [52, 36]. Before September 11 2001, the government's list of suspected terrorists banned from air travel totaled just 16 names. There are now over 44,000 passengers on the no-fly list, while the selectee list contains at least 75,000 names. Some of the most dangerous terrorists are never listed on either of the watch lists, as the intelligence agencies that supply the names do not want them circulated to airport employees in foreign countries for fear that they could end up in the hands of the terrorists [24].

Please use the following format when citing this chapter:

Soghoian, C., 2008, in IFIP International Federation for Information Processing, Volume 261; *Policies and Research in Identity Management*; Eds. E. de Leeuw, Fischer-Hübner, S., Tseng, J., Borking, J.; (Boston: Springer), pp. 5–21.

The concept of a no-fly list is premised on the idea that the government knowing who someone is can make airports safer. This idea is not universally accepted, and there are many researchers and commentators who strongly disagree with it [19]. In fact, the very definition of a "suicide bomber" means that there cannot be repeat offenders. This issue is beyond the scope of our paper as, useful or not, the US government wishes to have a no-fly list. We focus instead on the accuracy and effectiveness of the watch lists, and in highlighting the ways in which one can currently evade them.

The government's no-fly list is far from accurate [2]. It currently contains the names of 14 of the 19 September 11 hijackers and Saddam Hussein, all of whom are dead. It lists the name of convicted terrorist Zacarias Moussaoui, who is serving a life sentence in Colorado, and Evo Morales, the current elected president of Bolivia. Every flying passenger named Robert Johnson, Gary Smith or John Williams is subjected to an automatic and vigorous secondary screening, because at some point, suspected terrorists used these names as aliases. Even U.S. Senator Edward Kennedy found himself unable to fly for some time, although he was later able to personally demand that TSA clear his name. One reason for the high frequency of false positives for common names is because passengers are matched against the no-fly list by name only, instead of a combination of identity components such as date of birth, birthplace, current address or photograph [24].

Over 30,000 passengers have asked TSA to clear their names after being mistakenly linked to names on terror watch lists [31]. In January 2007, TSA Assistant Secretary Kip Hawley appeared before the US Congress to announce that the size of the no-fly list would be halved as a new more accurate list was introduced. He also announced that TSA was introducing a Traveler Redress Inquiry Program that will act as a central processing location for all passenger complaints that involve the no-fly and mandatory selectee lists [20].

TSA has been advocating for a number of years to be given the responsibility of checking passengers' names against the government watch lists, a task that airlines currently perform. Secure Flight is one of several attempts by TSA to perform airline passenger prescreening in-house. This program is intended to compare passenger information from Passenger Name Records, which contain information given by passengers when they book their flights, against watch lists maintained by the federal government [35]. The program, in development for over 4 years and at a cost of 140 million dollars, was suspended and sent back to the design stages in February of 2006 after investigators from the Congressional Goverment Accountability Office found that "TSA may not have proper controls in place to protect sensitive information" [4]. Assistant Secretary Hawley recently announced that the program is not expected to be complete until 2010, and that it will cost at least an additional 80 million dollars to develop and test [28].

Secure Flight was introduced shortly after the agency abandoned plans for its predecessor, the second generation Computer Assisted Passenger Prescreening System (CAPPS II). This scheme would have examined commercial and government databases to assess the risk posed by each passenger [22, 57]. CAPPS II was scheduled for a test run in the spring of 2003 using passenger data to be provided by Delta Airlines. Following a public outcry, however, Delta refused to provide the data and the test run was delayed indefinitely [16].

Having one's name on the no-fly list can be extremely dangerous. On September 26, 2002, Maher Arar, a Canadian software engineer changed flights in New York en route from Tunis to Montreal. He was detained by the United States Immigration and Naturalization Service, after his name came up in a database search due to misleading information supplied by the Royal Canadian Mounted Police. Even though he carried a Canadian passport, Arar was flown to Syria, against his will, where he was held in solitary confinement for over a year, and tortured regularly. After a year, the Syrian government concluded that he had no terrorist links and sent him back to Canada. Arar received a full apology from the Canadian Prime Minister in 2007, and received over 10 million dollars in compensation [29]. The US government insists that he has terrorist links, and has refused repeated requests from the Canadian government to remove him from the no-fly list.

Arar's experience highlights the most extreme consequences of appearing on the no-fly list. His experience and the more common experiences of passengers being delayed, detained or arrested [32], demonstrate the reasons why someone may want to evade an error prone watchlist plagued with false positives. However, the techniques for evading the no-fly list outlined in this paper are solely for domestic flights, and so even if he had known about them, Mr Arar would have been unable to use them.

2 Flying Without Identity Documents

There is no law or official regulation which requires that passengers show any identity document to a US government employee in order to board an airplane [44, 43]. TSA encourages travelers to have a government issued photo ID ready for inspection, yet its website does acknowledge an alternative option, stating that "the absence of proper identification will result in additional screening" [55]. TSA has repeatedly refused passengers' requests for the regulations detailing the ID policy. The government asserts that the rules are classified as Sensitive Security Information [25, 6], and are thus free from any requirement to be made public. This refusal prompted activist John Gilmore to file a lawsuit, which subsequently lead to the US Court of Appeals (9th Circuit) looking at the policies *in camera*. The judges summarized the policies in question, and thus, in theory, the right to fly without any ID in their opinion in *Gilmore v. Gonzales*, stating [18]:

> The identification policy requires that airline passengers either present identification or be subjected to a more extensive search. The more extensive search is similar to searches that we have determined were reasonable and consistent with a full recognition of appellants constitutional right to travel.

Passengers may be required to show identification to airline staff, but that is a private contractual matter between passengers and the airline. As such, the requirements tend to vary from airline to airline, based on their particular corporate policies [11, 10]. Through a combination of first-person testing by a number of activist passengers around the country [58, 33, 44, 56] and tests we have personally conducted, we have been able to piece together a picture of the ID requirements of a number of US airlines. Passengers have been able to successfully board domestic flights in the United States on multiple

airlines, including Northwest and United [45, 49], all without a single piece of identification. Other airlines require *some* form of identification. Passengers have been able
to board flights on Continental, Delta and American Airlines with identity documents
that include: prepaid credit cards purchased in cash, a library card and a hand-laminated
membership card to a local organic supermarket [47, 48, 56]. Passengers typically have
few if any problems when they claim to have forgotten their ID. However, passengers
who attempt to assert their right to fly without ID have at times, met stiffer resistance
from TSA [46, 30].

2.1 Interacting With The Airlines

Passengers are only required to interact with airline check-in staff when they wish to
"check" a bag - and have the airline take care of their luggage for them. If a passenger
is content to fly with just "carry on" items, she can quite easily make her way past the
TSA checkpoint and only ever encounter airline staff at the gate, before boarding the
airplane.

Any passenger that wishes to fly without approved identification documents must be
in possession of a boarding pass marked with the letters "SSSS" (Secondary Security
Screening Selectee), which instructs TSA staff to perform a more vigorous, or secondary search on the passenger. On some airlines, check-in staff can use their computer
terminals to print out special boarding passes that have the letters "SSSS" printed on
them [48, 45]. Other airlines simply have staff write the letters "SSSS" on the boarding
passes with an ink marker [47].

If a passenger approaches a TSA checkpoint without the approved identification
documents, and without a specially marked boarding pass, TSA are supposed to turn
the passenger away, and instruct them to obtain a special boarding pass from the airline
[47]. The legal hazards of testing the system have prevented us from attempting to go
through a TSA checkpoint with a self-marked boarding pass - and so, we cannot con-
clusively state that a passenger is able to do this. However, in addition to successfully
flying a number of times with "SSSS" boarding passes hand marked by airline staff, we
have also successfully gone through security with a boarding pass incorrectly marked
by the airlines: "SSS" instead of "SSSS", all without a single problem [47]. TSA staff
have no way of knowing who wrote the letters "SSSS" on a boarding pass. This is
mainly due to the fact that it is a hand-written addition to the boarding pass, which could
be added by any one of the hundreds of check-in employees who work at each airport.
There is not even an attempt to document the source of the "SSSS", through the use of
an employee's signature, initials or name.

If a nefarious passenger whose name appears on the no-fly list wishes to fly, the
simplest way for her to successfully board an airplane would be to purchase a ticket in
a fake name. If the passenger has booked a ticket on an airline that is relatively friendly
towards passengers that do not have ID, she should be able to claim forgotten ID and
request an "SSSS" boarding pass. If the passenger happens to be flying on an airline
with stricter rules, it may be more effective to print out a boarding pass at home, and
then hand-write the letters "SSSS" onto the boarding pass in a red ink pen - unless
she is willing to go through the trouble of procuring a fake library or student ID card
with which to prove her false identity to the airline. The passenger will be thoroughly

screened by TSA, and eventually allowed to board the plane. If her only goal is to evade the no-fly list, this simple technique should result in success.

We are not aware of any passenger who has successfully flown on a ticket purchased in a fake name, because testing this vulnerability may be illegal. However, a number of passengers have documented their experiences flying within the United States without showing a single piece of identification at the airport [49, 44]. Therefore, while we cannot state with the confidence that comes only through careful experimentation that this method of subverting the no-fly list is possible, it logically follows that it would.

3 Print-At-Home Passes

There are three varieties of boarding passes used by airlines. Those printed by airline check-in/gate staff, on official airline cardstock, those printed by unsupervised passengers using self-service check-in machines, and those printed out at home by passengers. This third type of boarding passes is the primary focus of this paper. It is quite possible that someone could make fraudulant tickets on couterfeit cardstock. With the help of an insider, it is also possible to produce documents on official airline stationary that listed fake information. Both of these threats are outside of the scope of this paper.

Print-at-home boarding passes were first introduced by Alaska Airlines in 1999, and have been in use by most US airlines since 2003. Usage rates vary by airline - as of 2006, 5 percent of eligible passengers on Delta Airlines print their boarding passes online, 9 percent at US Airways, 11 percent at NorthWest Airlines, and 15 percent usage amongst AirTran passengers [3]. Print-at-home boarding passes are much favored by both airlines and business travelers, their most frequent and profitable customers. A business passenger who has already printed out her own boarding pass and who is only traveling with carry-on baggage does not need to interact with airline staff until she has her pass scanned as she boards the airplane. This saves the airline a significant amount of money in labor and overhead costs, cuts down on average check-in time for other passengers who do require the help of an airline staff member, and reduces the amount of time that it takes for travelers to get through the airport and onto the airplane.

The online check-in process enables a passenger to login to the airline's website up to 24 hours before the flight, select seating, request an upgrade, enter their frequent flier number, and then finally, print out a dual human/machine-readable document - typically a combination of text, images and a barcode - from the comfort of their own home. Southwest Airlines famously does not allow passengers to reserve seats ahead of time, but allows passengers who check-in online to be amongst those who board the plane first, and thus get a chance at a window or aisle seat [27]. In an effort to further target business passengers, some airlines enable passengers to receive their boarding passes by fax [12, 34].

3.1 A No-Fly List Oracle

Most passengers can check-in online and print out their own boarding passes. International passengers are not able to print out their boarding passes at home, due to the legal requirement that airlines fully check their identity documents and verify that they have the necessary visa or passport to enter their destination country. While the airlines have a significant amount of flexibility for domestic passengers who lose or forget their ID, the rules for international passengers are far more strict.

Any domestic passenger whose name matches an entry in the no-fly list will be denied the option of printing a usable boarding pass at home [54]. Similarly, passengers who have been selected by the airline's computer systems for additional screening — due to the purchase of a one way ticket, a ticket paid in cash or a number of other suspicious behavior based triggers — will also need to present themselves to an airline staff member at the airport in order to obtain a valid boarding pass.

Researchers have previously noted that predictability in airport security systems is far worse than random searching. By traveling multiple times in advance of an attack, would-be terrorists can determine whether they are subject to different treatment. Those who are not selected for additional screening can be assigned to act. This ability to safely probe the watch lists through the use of "dry-runs" enables attackers to learn who amongst their team are likely to set off any passenger screening system alerts, all without jeopardizing their mission, or even risking jail [9]. Likewise, the ability to check-in online creates an easy to use oracle for learning who is and is not on the no fly list, from the comfort and safety of an anonymized Internet connection [14], a public library, or Internet cafe.

To verify if a name is or is not on the no-fly list, one can do the following:

1. Purchase a fully refundable ticket online in the name which one wishes to verify against the no-fly list (the subject).
2. Purchase a fully refundable ticket online in the name of a passenger who has recently flown without any problems (the control).
3. Attempt to check-in online less than 24 hours before the flight for both passengers.
4. Call the airline to cancel both tickets, and ask for a refund.

If one is able to successfully print out a valid boarding pass in the name of the control, but not the subject, it is quite likely that the subject's name is on the no-fly list. If, however, both passengers are denied the ability to print out a boarding pass online, it is far more likely that some other factor is triggering one of the secondary-screening rules.

4 Boarding Pass Systems

The airlines each employ differing and incompatible systems for the production and printing of online boarding passes. A large percentage of them do share at least one common property: They present the user with a html web page that contains all of the pertinent portions of the passenger record - first and last name, flight number, departure and destination cities, date, gate, etc - all in plain text, which can be saved and edited after the fact if a computer savvy user chooses to do so. Such passes typically include a handful of images. These include the airline's name or logo, and a computer readable barcode that will be scanned at the gate before the passenger boards the flight. Other airlines present the user with a single file, which contains all of the boarding pass information embedded in a single image. While this can also be modified with a graphical editing program such as Adobe Photoshop, it does require more effort and skill to modify than a text based html document [7].

Even when an airline produces a single-image based boarding pass, it is still possible for a motivated and technically skilled person to create a html based, and thus easily modifiable boarding pass that can pass for a real one. The goal of the attacker is typically not to produce a document that is 100% identical to the real article and able to withstand analysis by a trained forensics expert. It is rather to produce one that is good enough to pass the cursory check performed by a TSA employee, who sees several hundred similar documents every day.

The simplest method of producing a fake boarding pass is to use the html web page that the airline returns upon completion of online check-in. By saving this document locally, a user has everything she needs to produce documents good enough to get past current TSA checkpoints. Multiple websites have been created that automate this process, and allow anyone to print out a completely customizable yet authentic looking boarding pass. One of the sites was publicly shut down by the FBI (see figure 1) [23], while another remains online [1].

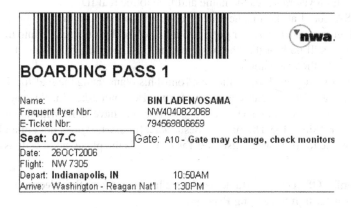

Fig. 1. A fake boarding pass created by a now shut-down website.

Bruce Schneier was the first to alert the public to this loophole in August of 2003. Since then, a number of commentators have written about the problem and all provide detailed instructions describing the process necessary to modify a print-at-home boarding pass [38, 3, 7, 39]. In particular, Senator Charles Schumer of New York has on multiple occasions provided step-by-step instructions for doing this on his official senate web site [40, 41].

Although these methods will allow someone to create a boarding pass good enough to get past security, the barcode included on each of these documents refers to a specific booking in the airline's reservation system. Any future attempted reuse of this barcode in a fake document will result in an invalid boarding pass, at least when presented to the airline employees at the gate. A passenger can get past the TSA checkpoint with one of these documents, as screening staff do not have the ability to access live passenger records, but it will not be enough to get aboard an airplane. To achieve that goal, a passenger whose name is on the no-fly list can use the combination of a genuine print-at-home boarding pass (purchased in a false name) with a fake boarding pass prepared at home. More importantly, she can do so while presenting her real identification documents, and will be able to avoid the rigorous and extensive screening procedures required when a passenger declines to show identification documents, as outlined earlier in this paper. Senator Schumer's instructions clearly explain this process [40]:

1. Joe Terror (whose name is on the terrorist watch list) buys a ticket online in the name of Joe Thompson using a stolen credit card. Joe Thompson is not listed on the terrorist watch list.
2. Joe Terror then prints his Joe Thompson boarding pass at home, and then electronically alters it (either by scanning or altering the original image, depending on the airline system and the technology he uses at home) to create a second almost identical boarding pass under the name Joe Terror, his name.
3. Joe Terror then goes to the airport and goes through security with his real ID and the FAKE boarding pass. The name and face match his real drivers license. The airport employee matches the name and face to the real ID.
4. The TSA guard at the magnetometer checks to make sure that the boarding pass looks legitimate as Joe Terror goes through. He/she does not scan it into the system, so there is still no hint that the name on the fake boarding pass is not the same as the name on the reservation.
5. Joe Terror then goes through the gate [onto] his plane using the real Joe Thompson boarding pass for the gates computer scanner. He is not asked for ID again to match the name on the scanner, so the fact that he does not have an ID with that name does not matter. [Since Joe Thompson doesnt actually exist, it does not coincide with a name on the terrorist watch list] Joe Terror boards the plane, no questions asked.

4.1 A Denial Of Service Attack Against The Transportation Security Administration Screening Process

In addition to enabling passengers to circumvent the no-fly list, the modifiable print-at-home boarding pass vulnerability can be used as an attack vector for other nefarious activities. Byers et. al. originally introduced the idea of an Internet-based attack against physical world resources in 2002 [8]. We now propose a similar attack against the TSA checkpoints at airports. Due to the significant legal risks involved in implementing this idea, we are unable to produce a proof-of concept. We are, however, able to explain it in some detail.

Every passenger whose boarding pass lists the letters "SSSS" is sent for secondary screening. Typically, their carry-on bags are emptied, searched, swabbed for chemical analysis, and in general, they are subjected to a significantly higher level of scrutiny than a typical passenger. They will also often be required to go through a physical pat-down by a TSA employee after walking through a magnetometer and or a chemical "puffer" machine. This experience commonly takes up to 10 minutes of at least one TSA agent's time, if not multiple agents.

The attack we propose requires a malicious software payload, which can be executed as a covert web-browser extension. This can be implemented using the Firefox Greasemonkey framework [37], or similar technologies for Microsoft Internet Explorer. Such a program will modify each html print-at-home boarding pass to add the letters "SSSS" to the pass in a highly visible place. There are a small enough number of domestic airlines in the Unites States that hard-coding the web site address of each airline's print-at-home boarding pass web page into a virus payload will not be too difficult. The technique will be particularly effective if it spreads across corporate networks, and worse, the public computer terminals at hotels used by business travelers.

Such a system will essentially force every infected passenger to be sent through an additional screening process. If distributed to enough computers, this will result in either significantly longer lines at the checkpoints and or significantly less attention being spent on each passenger undergoing the secondary screening process. The entire "SSSS" process is shrouded in such secrecy that passengers have no way of knowing if they will be selected under normal circumstances. It is therefore highly unlikely that travelers will associate their invasive search and delays at the airport with a potential software infection on their computer.

4.2   Boarding Pass Failures

Currently, the airlines are responsible for comparing a passenger's name against the government provided no-fly list. TSA must assume that if a passenger is in possession of a valid looking boarding pass, that their name has been compared against this list. If boarding passes can only be printed out by an airline employee after checking the ID of the passenger, the system remains reasonably secure. The no-fly list's integrity can be maintained even after the introduction of user-printed boarding passes, as long as the airlines compare each user's identity documents at the gate - and check ID's against the reservation in their computer system. Immediately after the September 11th 2001 terrorist attacks, this additional verification step was introduced. However, this check was later removed after complaints from the airlines that it caused additional delays to the boarding process [5].

When a passenger goes through a TSA checkpoint, several events occur. Assuming that the passenger presents some form of ID, TSA staff will compare the name on the ID to the name on the boarding pass. They will also check the time and date, departure airport name, and the terminal number. Staff will typically mark the boarding pass with an ink pen to certify that the passenger's identification documents have been checked. Other than by looking at the document, TSA employees have no way of verifying if the the boarding pass is real, valid, has been photocopied and used already that day or if it has been tampered with or modified by the would-be passenger.

TSA does not currently collect much data, if any at all. This is due to the fact that passenger's names are not recorded, nor is any information kept on the kind of identification presented. If asked after the fact, TSA will probably not be able to produce records listing when the passenger arrived at the checkpoint or how long it took to go through the checkpoint. If a checked-in passenger walks out of the airport 10 minutes before the plane departs, TSA will not know until the airline notifies them when their passenger count comes up short. This information may be obtainable after the fact through analysis of security camera tapes, but only if the authorities have a means of matching a face on film to a passenger record. It will certainly not be available in real-time.

5   Fixing The Problems

In response to the significant press coverage in the last year over the issue of fake boarding passes [23, 53], some commentators suggested that TSA should be given the means to check passengers' ID against the airlines' computer systems. Others continued to call for the airlines to restart the now-discontinued practice of checking ID's at the gate, a process that is still performed in Europe and elsewhere [42, 7, 41]

While having the airlines perform an ID check at the gate is the easiest solution to the main problem of user modified boarding passes, it does nothing to defend against the physical denial of service attack introduced earlier in this paper. In any case, it is a moot point, as the airlines clearly do not wish to bear the costs associated with an additional ID check before boarding. Thus, we now explore two alternative schemes that neutralize the modified boarding pass threat, the physical denial of service attack, allow TSA to perform the no-fly list check themselves as passengers pass through security, and enable the government to collect a wealth of live data on users as they pass through the security checkpoints.

Both schemes involve equipping TSA employees with handheld wireless devices, which are able to scan or photograph the barcodes printed on passengers' boarding passes.

5.1   A Naive Fix

The first solution requires that the airlines provide TSA with live access to their Passenger Name Record databases. Either the airlines will be required to agree upon a common data export standard, and therefore devote the resources required to modify their systems to use such a standard, or TSA will have to develop a system that can interface with each airline's unique database. Likewise, the airlines will either need to move to a common barcode standard for their boarding passes, or TSA will have to create software that can read the differing barcode schemes used by each airline. In addition to this time consuming and thoroughly expensive development process, the airlines will also have to expend significant resources to provide constant, live and secure access to their databases.

5.2   An Improved Fix

The main goal of a boarding pass verification system is to make it impossible to pass through the security checkpoint with a fake or modified boarding pass. There is no real need to give TSA live access to the airline's databases. TSA employees merely need a way of verifying that the boarding pass presented to them is valid and has not been modified in any way.

-----BEGIN PGP SIGNATURE-----
Version: GnuPG v1.2.1 (GNU/Linux)
Comment: See http://www.kernel.org/
signature.html for info

iD8DBQA/5WgqyGugaIF9Dw4RAjIiAJ0bz3q
+NGPPol3KTQ/NOVz8djN5+ACdEyvx
u1MeKSNI+5pOBjFxv63JPHk==CX+2i

-----END PGP SIGNATURE-----

Fig. 2. An OpenPGP signature encoded as a QRcode

In 2002, Lee et al. introduced the idea of using dense 2D barcodes to store digital signatures. They used the QRcode 2D matrix scheme (see figure 2), which can store up to 2,953 bytes of data per barcode. With current printing and reader technology, a 1024 bit signature can be printed in an area less than 10 mm sq [26]. The QRcode technology is already widely deployed in Japan. Barcodes are embedded in advertising posters, billboards, magazines and even fast food wrappers [51]. Most mobile phones on the Japanese market now include software that can scan the barcode using the built in camera phone. The barcode scheme is a clearly defined standard, with open source software development kits available as well as free, ready-to-use readers for Symbian OS and Java mobile phone devices [21].

We propose to embed all of the information typically printed on a boarding pass, along with a digital signature in a QRcode matrix. This can be produced by a software kit given to each airline. As all of the information to be contained in the barcode is already available at the time that the boarding pass is printed by the user, it should not require a significant engineering effort to use that same information to generate the barcode. There are a small enough number of domestic carriers in the United States that TSA can require each airline provide it with their barcode public key - and thus the airlines will simply self-sign their boarding pass barcodes. This negates any need for a central Public Key Infrastructure.

TSA personnel can thus be issued with a hand-held wireless computing device, capable of taking a photo of the barcodes. Screening staff will scan each 2D barcode-enabled boarding pass, after which, the software on the device will verify all of the information contained in the barcode, and using the public key given to TSA by the airline, will be able to verify that none of the information in the barcode has been tampered with or in any way modified since the barcode was produced.

All of the information needed to verify a boarding pass' authenticity is currently made available by the airlines at the time of boarding pass creation, so that the document can be printed out. No new information will be required of them. Thus, they are immediately freed of the requirement of providing live access to their databases to TSA.

If required, the airlines can publish a revocation list of the boarding passes that are no longer valid. Since boarding passes can only be printed at home within 24 hours of departure, it is quite likely that this list will remain rather small. The airlines can publish such a revocation list on their websites, or through some other public means, without risking any private passenger data, by only listing a unique barcode number associated with each boarding pass.

6   Improvements and Passenger Tracking

In both of these proposed schemes, TSA employees will be equipped with hand-held devices that scan the barcode on a boarding pass, and will display the passenger's information on the device's screen. By comparing the data on the screen (which will either be from the airline's database, or stored in the barcode and signed by the airline as original and unmodified) with the information on the passenger's identity documents, TSA agents will be able to completely do away with the threat of passenger modified boarding passes, as well as the risk posed by the physical denial of service attack introduced earlier in this paper. This is because TSA staff will not rely on the text printed on the boarding pass to learn a passenger's name, flight information and secondary screening status. They will instead be able to depend on a live database record or a digitally signed barcode to provide them with a trustworthy copy of that information.

As TSA agents will now have the passenger's name in a digital format as they go through the security checkpoint, it will be possible for TSA to take over the task of performing the no-fly list searches themselves. This will increase the security of the list, as it will no longer have to be shared with the airlines and will only be accessible by federal employees. Likewise, this will neutralize the at-home method of querying the no-fly list outlined in section 3.1 of this paper, as passengers will no longer be inadvertently told during online check-in if they are on the no-fly list or not.

Depending on the time required to query the no-fly list, the search can either happen as soon as the barcode is scanned, or, if more time is needed, the passenger's boarding pass can be scanned twice: once upon entering the security line — where the name will be read and submitted to a central database for comparison — and again once the passenger has passed through the metal detector, where the results of the search can be viewed to see if the passenger will be allowed to continue.

Many state drivers licenses already include information on the back of the license in a machine readable format, typically a barcode [13]. Were it required, such functionality can be added to TSA's hand-held devices, thus further reducing the amount of work that TSA staff are required to perform, and consequently, the possibility of human-related error. It is quite easy to imagine a scenario where a TSA employee scans the barcodes on the boarding pass and on the back of the passenger's drivers license, waits a few seconds as the system compares the passenger's name to the no-fly list, and then allows the passenger to pass after the system displays a message instructing the employee that the passenger is clear to fly.

In addition to simply checking a passenger's name against the no-fly list, TSA will now have a significant tool with which to collect real time data on passenger movement through airport terminals. They will be able to collect data on how long passengers arrive before their flights, how long it takes to get through the security checkpoint, assuming that the ID/pass is checked upon entering the line, and then again after the passenger goes through the magnetometer. Given that many state governments have monetized their drivers license databases [50, 15], it does not seem completely unrealistic to imagine a scenario where TSA will provide some of this data for sale. Airline food and concession vendors will probably be a fantastic market and would probably be very interested to know how long passengers spend captive in the airport, waiting for their flight to leave.

In the case that passengers are flying without ID, this system will at least enable TSA to lock a specific passenger ticket number as "used", and thus forbid multiple passengers without ID from passing through the checkpoint with a photocopy of the same print-at-home boarding pass. Were TSA to require that passengers leaving the secure area have their boarding passes scanned, this will also provide a key data source on the few passengers who leave the airport after clearing security, instead of boarding the flight. No doubt, TSA will probably like to identify and then question these passengers to discover the reason they were doing this, something that is not possible under the current system.

It is important to note that the system described in this paper will only fix the problem of fake or modified boarding passes. Even if TSA staff are equipped with hand-held devices, passengers will still be able to decline to show ID, and thus evade the no-fly list. This is not a problem that technology can solve, but is something that the US government must fix through policy changes, if it really wishes for a no-fly list to exist, and to be effectively enforced.

7 Conclusion

In this paper, we have outlined several problems with the enforcement and application of the no-fly list to domestic passengers in the United States. One of these problems is due to the fact that passengers can legally fly without showing any identity documents to US government employees, and can often fly without showing any such papers to airline staff. This problem remains open, and cannot be fixed without a change in policy by the US government.

We have also highlighted the problem of fake or user modified boarding passes, a problem which has been known, yet largely ignored by the government for a number of years. This issue has recently been the subject of a significant amount of press coverage, but as of now, remains unfixed. We introduced a method of determining if any particular name is on the no fly list, which one can perform safely and anonymously over the Internet. We introduced a physical denial of service attack against the TSA checkpoints at airports, distributed via an Internet virus.

We proposed two solutions to these problems, one naive yet expensive for the airlines, and another solution that retains many of the same security properties of the first, yet which is significantly cheaper. This second solution also frees the airlines of the costly and complicated need to provide live access to their passenger databases.

Both of these solutions will give TSA access to a wealth of live data on passengers activity in the airports, from the number of passengers at a particular checkpoint, the amount of time it takes a particular passenger to get through a checkpoint, to the amount of time a passenger waits in the departure area before boarding their flight. More importantly, both of the proposed solutions make the use of fake or modified print-at-home boarding passes impossible and will provide TSA with a means to check passenger's names against the no-fly list at the time they pass through security checkpoints.

Acknowledgements

Many thanks to Kelly Caine, John Doyle, Virgil Griffith, Kristin Hanks, Markus Jakobsson and Katherine Townsend for their helpful comments. Sid Stamm provided both helpful feedback and helped to flesh out the idea of the boarding pass virus discussed in section 4.1.

References

1. John Adams. Document gennreator [sic], November 1 2006. http://j0hn4d4m5.bravehost.com/.
2. American Civil Liberties Union. Frequently Asked Questions About the "No Fly List", October 26 2005. http://www.aclu.org/safefree/general/21164res20051026.html.
3. Anonymous. Airport Security's Achilles' Heel. *CSO: The Resourcec for Security Executives*, February 01 2006. http://www.csoonline.com/read/020106/caveat021706.html.
4. Associated Press. TSA's Secure Flight program suspended, February 09 2006. http://www.msnbc.msn.com/id/11254968/.
5. Matt Blaze. Human-scale security and the TSA, January 01 2007. http://www.crypto.com/blog/tsa_paranoia.
6. Sara Bodenheimer. Super Secret Information? The Discoverability Of Sensitive Security Information As Designated By The Transportation Security Administration. *UMKC L. Rev.*, 73:739, Spring 2005.
7. Andy Bowers. A dangerous loophole in airport security. *Slate Magazine*, February 07 2005. http://www.slate.com/id/2113157/.
8. Simon Byers, Aviel D. Rubin, and David Kormann. Defending against an internet-based attack on the physical world. *ACM Trans. Inter. Tech.*, 4(3):239–254, 2004.
9. Samidh Chakrabarti and Aaron Strauss. Carnival booth: An algorithm for defeating the computer-assisted passenger screening system. *First Monday*, 7(10), 2002. http://firstmonday.org/issues/issue7_10/chakrabarti/index.html.
10. Jayen Clark. Just who do you think you are, without ID? *USA Today*, April 28 2005. http://www.usatoday.com/travel/news/2005-04-28-travel-ids_x.htm.
11. Continental Airlines. ID Requirements, 2007. http://www.continental.com/web/en-us/content/travel/airport/id/default.aspx.
12. Continental Airlines. Online Check-in FAQ, 2007. http://www.continental.com/web/en-US/content/help/onlinecheckin.aspx.
13. John T. Cross. Age Verification In The 21st Century : Swiping Away Your Privacy. *John Marshall J. of Comp. & Info. Law*, 23(2), Winter 2005.
14. Roger Dingledine, Nick Mathewson, and Paul Syverson. Tor: The second-generation onion router. In *Proceedings of the 13th USENIX Security Symposium*, August 2004. http://tor.eff.org/tor-design.pdf.

15. Serge Egelman and Lorrie Faith Cranor. The Real ID Act: Fixing Identity Documents with Duct Tape. *I/S: A Journal of Law and Policy for the Information Society*, 2(1):149–183, Winter 2006.

16. Electronic Privacy Information Center. EPIC Secure Flight Page, February 09 2006. http://www.epic.org/privacy/airtravel/secureflight.html.

17. Justin Florence. Making The No Fly List Fly: A Due Process Model For Terrorist Watchlists. *Yale Law Journal*, 115(8):2148–2181, June 2006.

18. *Gilmore v. Gonzales*. 04-15736 (9th Cir. 2006). http://www.papersplease.org/gilmore/_dl/GilmoreDecision.pdf.

19. Jim Harper. *Identity Crisis: How Identification Is Overused and Misunderstood*, chapter 23, page 215. CATO Institute, Washington, DC, 2006.

20. Kip Hawley. Prepared statement. *U.S. Senate Committee on Commerce, Science and Transportation*, January 17 2007. http://www.tsa.gov/press/speeches/air_cargo_testimony.shtm.

21. Kaywa Reader. What is the Kaywa Reader, 2006. http://reader.kaywa.com/faq/25.

22. Leigh A. Kite. Red Flagging Civil Liberties and Due Process Rights of Airline Passengers: Will a Redesigned CAPPS II System Meet the Constitutional Challenge? *Wash. & Lee L. Rev.*, 61(3), Summer 2004.

23. Brian Krebs. Student Unleashes Uprorar With Bogus Airline Boarding Passes. *The Washington Post*, November 1 2006. http://www.washingtonpost.com/wp-dyn/content/article/2006/10/31/AR2006103101313.html.

24. Steve Kroft. Unlikely terrorist on no fly list. *60 Minutes*, October 8 2006. http://www.cbsnews.com/stories/2006/10/05/60minutes/printable2066624.shtml.

25. Linda L. Lane. The Discoverability of Sensitive Security Information in Aviation Litigation. *Journal of Air Law and Commerce*, 71(3):427–448, Summer 2006.

26. Jaeil Lee, Taekyoung Kwon, Sanghoon Song, and JooSeok Song. A model for embedding and authorizing digital signatures in printed documents. In *ICISC*, pages 465–477, 2002.

27. Ron Lieber and Susan Warren. Southwest Makes It Harder To Jump the Line. *The Wall Street Journal*, June 7 2006. http://online.wsj.com/article/SB114964168631673304.html.

28. Eric Lipton. U.S. Official Admits to Big Delay in Revamping No-Fly Program. *The New York Times*, February 21 2007. http://www.nytimes.com/2007/02/21/washington/21secure.html.

29. Andrew Mayeda and Sheldon Alberts. Harper offers Arar apology – and $10M. *The Star Phoenix*, January 27 2007. http://www.canada.com/saskatoonstarphoenix/news/story.html?id=441709d5-8eea-4588-ab00-902b748408d2.

30. Declan McCullagh. Airport ID checks legally enforced? *CNET News.com*, December 8 2005. http://news.com.com/Airport+ID+checks+legally+enforced/2100-7348_3-5987820.html.

31. Leslie Miller. Report: Thousands Wrongly on Terror List. *The Associated Press*, October 6 2006. http://www.washingtonpost.com/wp-dyn/content/article/2006/10/06/AR2006100601360.html.

32. Mima Mohammed and Jenny Allen. Grad files national suit. *The Stanford Daily*, February 16 2006. http://daily.stanford.edu/article/2006/2/16/gradFilesNationalSuit.

33. Eric Nguyen. No ID, June 12 2006. http://mindtangle.net/2006/06/12/no-id/.

34. Northwest Airlines. Press Release: Northwest Expands Boarding Pass Faxing Service to International Locations, October 19 2006. http://news.thomasnet.com/companystory/496855.

35. Yousri Omar. Plane Harassment: The Transportation Security Administration's Indifference To The Constituion In Administering The Government's Watch Lists. *Wash. & Lee J. Civil Rts. & Soc. Just.*, 12(2), Spring 2006.

36. Soumya Panda. The Procedural Due Process Requirements for No-Fly Lists. *Pierce L. Rev.*, 4(1), December 2005.

37. Mark Pilgrim. What is greasemonkey, May 9 2005. http://diveintogreasemonkey.org/install/what-is-greasemonkey.html.

38. Ryan. Changing A Southwest Boarding Pass, July 30 2006. http://boardfast.blogspot.com/2006/07/how-to-change-southwest-airlines.html.

39. Bruce Schneier. Flying on Someone Else's Airplane Ticket. *Crypto-Gram*, August 15 2003. http://www.schneier.com/crypto-gram-0308.html#6.

40. Charles Schumer. Schumer reveals new gaping hole in air security, February 13 2005. http://www.senate.gov/~schumer/SchumerWebsite/pressroom/press_releases/2005/PR4123.aviationsecurity021305.html.

41. Charles Schumer. Schumer Reveals: In Simple Steps Terrorists Can Forge Boarding Pass And Board Any Plane Without Breaking The Law!, April 09 2006. http://www.senate.gov/~schumer/SchumerWebsite/pressroom/record.cfm?id=259517.

42. Adam Shostack. On Printing Boarding Passes, Christopher Soghoian-style. Emergent Chaos, October 28 2006. http://www.emergentchaos.com/archives/2006/10/on_printing_boarding_pass.html.

43. Ryan Singel. Fliers can't balk at search. *Wired News*, March 20 2006. http://www.wired.com/news/technology/1,70450-0.html.

44. Ryan Singel. The Great No-ID Airport Challenge. *Wired News*, June 9 2006. http://www.wired.com/news/technology/0,71115-0.html.

45. Christopher Soghoian. Slight Paranoia: TSA Love, September 21 2006. http://paranoia.dubfire.net/2006/09/tsa-love.html.

46. Christopher Soghoian. ID rules inna Babylon: A police confrontation at DCA Airport, February 19 2007. http://paranoia.dubfire.net/2007/02/id-rules-inna-babylon-police.html.

47. Christopher Soghoian. Slight Paranoia: A clearer picture of how to fly with no ID, January 21 2007. http://paranoia.dubfire.net/2007/01/clearer-picture-of-how-to-fly-with-no.html.

48. Christopher Soghoian. Slight Paranoia: Much fun at SFO airport, January 29 2007. http://paranoia.dubfire.net/2007/01/much-fun-at-sfo-airport.html.

49. Christopher Soghoian. Slight Paranoia: No ID on United: Piece of Cake, February 02 2007. http://paranoia.dubfire.net/2007/02/no-id-on-united-piece-of-cake.html.

50. Daniel J. Solove. Access And Aggregation: Public Records, Privacy And The Constitution. *Minn. L. Rev.*, 86:1137, June 2002.

51. Spark Productions. Japanese QR codes provide marketers a glimpse of the future. *Japan Marketing News*, January 17 2007. http://www.japanmarketingnews.com/2007/01/in_previous_art.html.

52. Daniel J. Steinbock. Designating The Dangerous: From Blacklists To Watch Lists. *Seattle Univerity Law Review*, 30(Issue 1), Fall 2006.

53. Randall Stross. Theater of the Absurd at the T.S.A. *The New York Times*, December 17 2006. http://www.nytimes.com/2006/12/17/business/yourmoney/17digi.html.

54. Transportation Security Administration. TRIP: Traveler Identity Verification Form, February 20 2007. `https://trip.dhs.gov/`.
55. Transportation Security Administration. TSA: Our Travelers: What you need, February 13 2007. `http://www.tsa.gov/travelers/airtravel/screening/index.shtm#5`.
56. Siva Vaidhyanathan. Can you board a plane without ID?, March 24 2006. `http://www.nyu.edu/classes/siva/archives/002939.html`.
57. Deborah von Rochow-Leuschner. CAPPS II and the Fourth Amendment: Does It Fly? *Journal of Air Law and Commerce*, 69(1):139–173, Winter 2004.
58. David Wagner. Flying without ID, October 20 2000. `http://www.cs.berkeley.edu/~daw/faa/noid.html`.

Privacy and Identity Management

Context Based Enforcement of Authorization for Privacy and Security in Identity Management*

Vasu Alagar[1] and Kaiyu Wan[1]

[1] Concordia University
Montreal, Canada
alagar@cs.concordia.ca
[2] East China Normal University
Shanghai, P.R.C
kaiyu.wan@gmail.com

Abstract. Protecting the identity of an individual is a shared responsibility between the individual, the organizations with whom the individual will be transacting during her life time, and the state of which the individual is a legal resident. Identity theft occurs when someone uses an individual's personal information without the knowledge of the individual to commit a crime, such as fraud or theft. Of late identity theft has become one of the fastest growing crimes, not only in western countries but also in developing countries where internet dominates business, financial transactions of big organizations, and social activities of individuals. In this paper we discuss a context based enforcement of authorization to protect the privacy of individuals and secure information about them stored in large identity management systems.

1 Introduction

Privacy and security are complementary issues. From an individual's point of view privacy is paramount. From an organization's point of view security is a quality of service (QoS) requirement. In practice, it is required to protect the identity of an individual (honoring her privacy), while at the same time revealing information of that individual to another individual who is authorized to get such information. In several countries privacy is regarded as a fundamental right and is implemented in state legislation. To assure privacy of an individual and to decide who is authorized to get a specific information about that individual, *identity* is the common factor.

The *identity* of a person is established at birth and it may exist even after the death of a person. At birth, the birth *certificate* records the place and date of birth of the child, the name(s) given to the child, the identities of her legal parents, and any identifiable physical marks of the child. This certificate, issued by a *trusted authority* who is authorized by the state to issue it, establishes the identity of the child. At death, the death certificate is issued which in principle should make a *reference* to the birth certificate of the deceased. The death certificate does not necessarily annul the birth certificate but

*The research is supported by a grant from Natural Sciences and Engineering Research Council, Canada.

Please use the following format when citing this chapter:

Alagar, V. and Wan, K., 2008, in IFIP International Federation for Information Processing, Volume 261; *Policies and Research in Identity Management*; Eds. E. de Leeuw, Fischer-Hübner, S., Tseng, J., Borking, J.; (Boston: Springer), pp. 25–37.

only disassociates the identity of the person from the person, because the person no longer exists. In between birth and death, more and more certificates may be issued to a person by various trusted organizations and government agencies of the country where the person lives. Different certificates of the individual are normally used to establish the identity of the person at different *contexts*. We formalize the context notion in Section 2.2. Until then we use the term "context", as defined in Oxford English Dictionary: *context defines the circumstances that form the setting for an event.*

We distinguish between *credential* and certificate: a certificate of a person is a declarative statement which is true at all times, whereas a credential presented by a requester is a document which should *prove* beyond doubt the identity of the presenter to an *authority* who at the context of its presentation is responsible to enforce certain *policies*. Examples of automated systems that use credentials to establish the identity are electronic voting systems, on-line banking systems, and on-line health care systems. A typical scenario in completing a transaction in such systems involves three steps: (1) a client (subject) submits a request, usually supported by a set of *credentials*; (2) the system applies the current policy to the submitted credentials to establish the identity of the user, and validates whether or not the user has the rights to receive the requested resources; (3) the system applies the security and privacy policy in servicing the request, if step 2 is successful. Thus, identity management in a system requires the management of a policy base and an automated procedure for applying policies at different contexts.

A policy is a *rule* that applies to some scenario in the daily life-cycle of the organization's activity. Broadly, the rules can be classified into *business rules* and *security rules*. Business rules describe terms and conditions, service provisions, contracts and their execution. Typically, a work-flow specification in an organization is driven by business rules. On the other hand, security rules set restrictions on access to resources and regulate information flow. Security policies are domain-specific, restricting access to objects in that domain. When an organization sets up a system to automate identity management, the application of a policy defines a certain choice in the behavior of the system. It is important to separate the policy from the system implementation, in order to allow the policy to be modified which in turn can dynamically alter the system behavior, without changing the system implementation. In this paper we explain how this may be achieved using contexts.

The main contributions of this paper are: (1) security contexts for enforcing security; (2) policy base organization as a rule-based system with context condition attached to each rule; (3) a formal approach to automate authorization and secure service provision.

2   Notation and Concepts

In this section we make precise three basic concepts and give their abstract view. By a system we mean a set of policies PB, interacting *subjects (entities)* S, and a set of *objects (resources)* O controlled by subjects. The *status* of a subject $s \in S$ at any time in the system is one of the following: (i) s is an individual subject; (ii) s belongs to one or more groups; or (iii) s plays a set of roles with or without group membership.

2.1   Identity of an Entity

It is commonly understood [2] that the identity of an individual comprises a set of personal information about the person. We try to make this concept as precise as possible. Determining the identity of an entity x arises whenever it enters into a transaction which in turn requires access to a resource o controlled by another entity y. The requester x must provide sufficient credentials to y so that y can establish the identity of x and then determine the type of access that can be granted for x over o. The task of determining the identity is called *authentication*. Knowing the identity of the requester, the act of granting appropriate access to o is based on access control policy. Authorization is authentication *plus* granting access.

In traditional systems, which are closed systems, the requester is identified by the system because the credentials are known only to each other. However, in many internet applications the resource owner, who has to authorize, and the requester are unknown to one another. The requester may want to remain anonymous and present only a minimum amount of information, which may be a partial set of credentials furnished by third parties. Based on the submitted credentials the system has to decide whether or not to authorize the request. Below is a typical scenario arising in on-line banking systems.

Example 1 *Alice has a checking account with ABC bank and is privileged to use the bank's on-line banking facility. She is given a 14 digit account number and has chosen a password to go with it. The personal information of Alice, collected by the bank at the time of opening the account, is saved under her personal profile. She has also recorded with the bank a set of skill-testing questions and her answers for the questions. Assume that whenever she uses her personal computer at home to access the banking facilities, her account number and password combination is accepted by the system as proof of her identity. Once on her travel, let her access the on-line facility using the computer in her hotel room. After her usual log-in session, she may get a message "the system is unable to identify you", and direct her to contact the bank either in person or through telephone. Why her identity is not authenticated? A possible answer is that the bank's online system uses a whole lot of information that it has collected and saved in the system file to authorize her. When she accesses the system from the hotel computer, the system infers non-compliance with her access history and decides not to authorize her. Another possible scenario is when she accesses the system from a hotel room or internet cafe in her later travels: the system, instead of denying her service, may try harder to prove her identity. The system may interrogate her with one or more randomly chosen skill-testing questions saved in her profile. The system will allow her access if her response to the query matches the answer stored in her profile. Hence, the system will require different sets of credentials to be presented at different contexts in order to authenticate its user.*

Based on the above discussions we propose a definition of identity:

Definition 1 *A certificate is a declaration about an entity or an object, issued by a trusted authority, who is not the entity. A credential is a declaration of an entity about an entity (possibly self-referencing). A certificate is a credential. The identity of an entity at any context is a non-empty subset of certificates accumulated by the entity until that* *context. Authentication in a context is the proof of compliance that the credentials that are presented by an entity in the context are sufficient to establish the identity of the entity in that context.*

2.2 Context

We use the definition of context given in [7], in particular use their definition and notation for security contexts. To understand the need to formalize context, let us consider the policy *Policy1: A physician on-duty in a hospital can access the medical records of patients either admitted by her or treated by her.* This policy refers to physician name, her current status (on-duty or off-duty), patients admitted by her, and patients under her care. The context for enforcing the policy is suggested by the above information. Notice that the context information is *multidimensional*, and is determined by the four dimensions PN (a finite set of physician names), PS (a finite set of statuses of physicians), WS (a finite collection of work schedules), PA (a finite set of patients admitted) and PC (a finite set of patients cared). Associated with each dimension there exists a finite set of values, called tags, as indicated above. An example of a context c with these dimensions is represented in the syntax $[PN : Bob, PS : on - duty, WS : 1, PA : Alice, PC : Tom]$. This context describes the setting in which "physician Bob is on duty on the first day of the week, admitted Alice and cared for Tom". "Policy1" can be applied to this context to validate Bob for accessing medical records, as well as track the flow of information of the patient records. What is important is to make clear that "Alice" and "Tom" are patients and not hospital personnel. That is, context definition requires a unique dimension name for each entity type, because a hospital patient may also be an employee in the hospital.

The security context types introduced in [7] are useful for representing rules in the policy base and for enforcing policies. Let us briefly comment on how and where they fit in our work. Three security categories proposed in [7] are *Internal Security Category*(ISC), *Boundary Security Category*(BSC), and *External Security Category*(ESC). A context in ISC category specifies the authorization for one user to access data in one category. An example of ISC context is $[UC_1 : u, DC_2 : j, PC : Legal]$, meaning that user u with role UC_1 is allowed to access the data (resource) type j in category DC_2 for legal purposes. This context type is useful for the access policy that specifies "which entity can access a resource and for what purpose". A context in BSC category specifies the configuration of fire wall security for each user category. An example of BSC context is $[NAME : Alice, SP : NULL, IF : vlan100, IF : vlan120, CLASS : gold, CURL : root]$. The BSC contexts are usually configured by the system administrator to optimize resource utilization and system protection. This context configured at the fire wall authenticates remote users and directs their requests through interfaces that can apply the access policies. A context in ESC category specifies the contextual information governing the user's request. An example of ESC context is $[LOC : Berlin, TIME : d_1, WHO : Alice, WHAT : filetransfer, WHERE : Paris, WHEN : d_2, WHY : Auditing]$. This context type is relevant for monitoring "data transfer" policies.

For an efficient representation and retrieval of rules from the policy base we associate with a context of one type a set of contexts of another type. We may call this association *lifting*. Intuitively, a context c and a context c' that is lifted from it have something in common: a policy that is valid in context c may also be valid in context c'. Usually, contexts c and c' will have some common dimensions or same tag types of some of the dimensions in c are the same as those of some dimensions in c', although the two dimension sets are different. Lifting is used in Section 2.3 for constructing security contexts and in Section 4.1 for linking related policies.

2.3 Access Policy and Grant Policy

We modify the grant policy defined in traditional systems in order to make it context-specific. Abstractly, we define access policies by functions: (1) Function AS assigns to an individual $s \in S$ a set of signed actions, called *access rights*, on an object $o \in O$. If $+a \in AS(s,o)$, then the subject s is allowed to perform action a on object o; however, if $-a \in AS(s,o)$, then the subject s is not allowed to perform action a on the object o. If neither $+a$ nor $-a$ is $\in AS(s,o)$, the access policy is undefined for subject s on object o. (2) Function AG assigns to a group $g \in G$ a set of rights on an object $o \in O$. The function SG gives for a subject s the groups $SG(s)$ to which the subject s belongs. (3) Function SR gives for each individual subject $s \in S$, the set $SR(s)$ of roles assumed by s. The function AR defines for each role $r \in R$, the set $AR(r,o)$ of rights that r has on the object o.

We define the grant policy as a function SP, which for a subject s in context c grants or denies access to object o. We use the notation $PB@c$ to mean "the evaluation of policy base PB at context c". The result of evaluation is either a successful validation (true) or an unsuccessful validation (false). In the former case a non-empty subset of PB, rules that are applicable for context c, is also retrieved from the policy base. Section 5 explains $PB@c$ in detail.

1. [P1:] *s is an individual subject* The subject s is granted to perform the actions explicitly allowed for it on the object o if there exists no policy in context c that overrules that privilege . $SP(s,o,c) = if\ PB\ @\ c\ then\ AS(s,o)\ else\ \emptyset$

2. [P2:] *s has a set of roles but is not a member of a group* The subject s is granted the right to perform an action a on an object o in context c if at least one of the roles in $SR(s) \neq \emptyset$ is authorized to access o and none of them is denied to access o in context c. $SP(s,o,c) = \{+a \mid p_r(a,s,o) \wedge a \in A \wedge r \in SR(s)\}$, where
   $p_r(a,s,o) \equiv PB\ @\ c \wedge\ +a \in AR(r,o)\ \wedge\ \sim \exists r' \in SR(s) \bullet (-a \in AR(r',o))$.

3. [P3:] *s has no roles and belongs to one or more groups* In context c the subject s belonging to the groups in $SG(s)$ is granted to perform an action a on an object o, if at least one of the groups in $SG(s)$ is authorized to access o in context c and none of the groups in $SG(s)$ is denied to access it in context c. $SP(s,o,c) = \{+a \mid p_g(a,s,o) \wedge a \in A \wedge g \in SG(s)\}$, where
   $p_g(a,s,o) \equiv PB\ @\ c \wedge\ +a \in AG(g,o) \wedge \sim \exists g' \in SG(s) \bullet (-a \in AG(g',o))$.

4. [P4:] *s has a set of roles and belongs to one or more groups* Using the predicates defined in the previous two steps we define $SP(s,o,c) = \{+a \mid p_r(a,s,o) \wedge a \in A \wedge r \in SR(s)\} \cup \{+a \mid p_g(a,s,o) \wedge a \in A \wedge g \in SG(s)\}$

The grant policy is applied only if a request is successfully validated. The procedure for validating a request at the security contexts is as follows: (1) *Fire wall*- From the user request, an ESC context associated with the request is extracted. A BSC context is constructed by "lifting" the ESC context. (2) *Authorization:System Access-* One of the servers in the interface IF of the BSC context should authenticate the user. If the authentication fails service is denied. If the authentication succeeds the security policy SP of the context is applied. The result of this application is either "Allow" or "Deny". If the permission is granted, the request is taken up for internal processing. (3) *Access/Grant-* An ISC context is constructed from the ESC and BSC contexts and the grant policy is applied in this context. The next example illustrates this procedure.

Example 2 *Let* $[LOC : Berlin, TIME : d_1, WHO : Alice, WHAT :$
filetransfer, WHERE : Paris, WHEN : d_2, WHY : Auditing] be the ESC context constructed from a request made by Alice. The dimension WHO from ESC is mapped to the dimension $NAME$ in BSC, partially constructing $[NAME : Alice]$. This step is justified because these two dimensions have the same tag set. The dimensions $LOC, WHERE, WHAT, WHY$ from ESC taken together are mapped onto the dimension SP in BSC. That is because the policy for transferring a file is relevant for the context defined by these dimensions. The part of that policy, say p, that is relevant to the interface is assigned to SP. Thus, the constructed context $[NAME : Alice]$ is extended to $[NAME : Alice, SP : p]$. From the name Alice and the fire wall configuration policy for user categories, the system will determine the rest of the dimensions $IF, CLASS,$ and $CURL$, and complete the construction of the BSC context corresponding to the ESC context. This step may fail. If it fails, the request is not validated at the fire wall. If the validation is successful the ISC context is constructed. The system constructs the context $c' = [WHO : Alice, WHAT : filetransfer, WHY : Auditing]$ by first mapping $NAME$ to WHO, next mapping the dimensions $CLASS$ and $NAME$ from BSC of context c' to the dimension UC_i of ISC, and finally maps the dimension $WHAT$ and WHY from context c' respectively to the dimensions DC_2 and PC. Thus, it constructs the ISC context $[UC_i : Alice, DC_j : filetransfer, PC : Auditing]$. The grant policy for Alice on the particular object file to be transferred is evaluated at this context.

3   Threats and Safeguards

There are three sources of threat: *personal life style, organizational*, and *systemic*. Many institutions and governments have set up web sites to warn individuals about identity theft and how it can prevented through a disciplined life style. See [8–10] for information posted from North American and European government agencies warning individuals about identity theft and what should be done to prevent it. The two primary sources of organizational threats are employees of the organization who manage the database, and outside attackers. The first kind of threat arises when some employees use illegitimate means and violate local policies to access the information which is not legitimately required in their job related tasks. Some of the disclosures that happen inside are "accidental". As an example, the information left on the screen of a computer can be seen by another employee who is not authorized to know it. Some simple remedies include automatic log-outs whenever the system is left idle, and reminding employees about their behavioral code. Another kind of threat is that employees who have authorized access violate the trust instituted in them. As an example, an employee may be curious to know a particular individual's date of birth or marital status. A remedy is to protect confidential data through encryption, authentication based on public key cryptography, and electronic signature. Another kind of threat is due to collaboration among a group of employees to access data on an individual, which cannot be accessed individually. Rotating employees to work in different groups, and audit trails seem the best way to deter this kind of threat. An individual who has no physical access and not an authorized user in an organization is a threat when the security perimeter of the organization is compromised. As an example, an intruder from one city might gain authorization to a financial institution in another city and obtain the identities of all millionaires in that city. Another example is when an outsider is able to infect the files in the system with virus, which make the system loose its valuable information or crash. A remedy is to strengthen fire walls, use encryption to protect the confidentiality and integrity of vital data, and safe-keeping back up tapes in encrypted form.

Systemic concerns are rooted in the procedures followed for using personal information by various agencies. Information flows across different domains, where the policies for accessing and using the information in different domains are in general different. The fact is that policies in one domain may not be known to other domains. Consequently, policies in different domains do not add up to a comprehensive global policy that will protect the privacy or the identity of the individual. As an example, the personal information of a person who is admitted to a hospital is shared by physicians, health care providers, insurers, and government agencies who provide Medicare. We contend that ESC context can be used effectively to protect personal information.

Suppose a subject s_1 in domain d_1 sends some information to a subject s_2 in domain d_2. An ESC context is constructed for this request at the periphery of the domain d_2. This context must include "the purpose" of the request. Since "purpose" is a domain information, it will be assigned a security level clearance. Consequently, the transmission channel through which the request is sent must have a security clearance higher than or equal to that assigned for the "purpose" category. Moreover, the subject s_1 should have the security clearance for sending the request, and s_2 in domain d_2 must have the security clearance to receive the request. The security level clearances within a domain is confidential to that domain, and consequently it is not possible to compare security level clearances in different domains. However, the medium used to communicate is common for both domains. Therefore it seems appropriate to assume that the security level assigned to the communication channel between the domains is known to both domains. Assume that security levels are modeled by functions slc and olc, where $slc(s)$ gives the *security level clearance* for the subject $s \in S$, and $olc(o)$ gives the *security level classification* for the object $o \in O$. Based on this premise, we impose three constraints for a secure information flow from s_1 to s_2 while sending data o along a channel α.

(1) [secure channel for object o]: $olc(o) \leq olc(\alpha)$
(2) [s_1 can write on α]: $slc(s_1) \leq olc(\alpha)$
(3) [s_2 can read, not write on α]: $slc(s_2) \geq olc(\alpha)$

4 Public Policy Framework - a proposal

A policy mentions subjects, objects (resources), roles, and suggests either directly or indirectly a sequence of actions to be done when the rule is followed. Policies govern the sets S, O, G, and R that exist across different domains. We assume that each group is associated with a distinguished subject, called *leader*, who ensures that policies are followed in all transactions engaged by the group. In a computerized system, this leader can be realized by an *agent*.

4.1 Policy Representation

A policy in every domain is a rule. An example policy is *a physician will have access to medical information on the patients under her care*. A policy, being a declarative statement, does not dictate how it should be represented in organizational databases and how it should be implemented. However we recommend that the policy representation include information on where it is applicable. A policy is represented by a rule $H \Leftarrow B$, where H is called the *head (consequent)* of the rule and B is called the *body (antecedent)* of the rule. In general, the body of a rule is a conjunction of one or more conditions; no disjunction is allowed in the body. The head of a rule, expressed declaratively, is an action specification. We associate a context condition U with each rule to suggest that the rule is applicable in any context that satisfies this condition. This is a major difference between our approach and others [3, 5, 4] who have developed languages for policy specification and application. By separating the context condition from the rule we achieve rule generality, and flexibility in the application of the rule.

Example 3 *Consider the rule* $U : has\_record(x, y, z) \Leftarrow patient(y, z) \wedge attends(x, y) \wedge staff(x, z)$, *where* $U = (physician(x) \wedge service(x) \geq 5) \vee head\_nurse(x) \vee secretary(x) \wedge admits(x, y, z)$ *is the context condition. The meaning of the rule is* "a staff x attending on a patient y in department z has access to the patient record within the department", *and the context condition provides the different contexts in which this rule can be applied, namely* "a physician with 5 or more years of experience is attending the patient, or a head nurse of that department, or the secretary who admits the patient in that department".

In general, a policy database may be large. For an efficient processing of transactions, we propose two methods to organize the rules.

Partitioning Policy Base The set BP of rules is partitioned so that each subset has policies associated with a specific domain. The function DP defines for each domain $d \in D$, the set $DP(d) \subset BP$ of rules that are relevant to that domain. Denoting the domain that is specific to the subject s by s_d, $d \in D$, the set $DP(s_d)$ gives the set of rules to be followed by s. In general, a group $g \in G$ may be responsible to deal with business transactions in more than one domain. The function RD defines for each group $g \in G$, the set $RD(g)$ of domains for business transactions. The set of rules to be followed by individual s belonging to group g, as well the rules that must be enforced by the leader of the group $g \in G$ is $BR(g) = \bigcup_{d \in RD(g)} DP(d)$. An advantage of partitioning is that each partition contains domain specific rules.

Linking Partitions For every pair of domains $d_i, d_j \in D, d_i \neq d_j$, we define a lifting function ϕ_{ij}, that associates with a rule $r \in DP(d_i)$ a subset $\phi_{ij}(r) \subset DP(d_j)$. The interpretation is that for the rule $r \in DP(d_i)$, the set of rules $\phi_{ij}(r)$ belonging to $DP(d_j)$ are *relevant*. This association is important in tracing the information flow from a source in domain d_i to a source in domain d_j. We define relevance in terms of the context condition:

A rule $r :: U : H \Leftarrow B$ is relevant to the rule $r' :: U' : H' \Leftarrow B'$ if $U' \rightarrow U$.

Informally, if the context condition U' *implies* the context condition U, then a policy enforced in a context defined by U is quite relevant in a context defined by U' and should be enforced there. Thus, every rule $r \in PB$ that is relevant to the rule $r' \in PB$ has a link in it that is directed from r' to r. When a rule changes, the policy base must be updated. However, when a rule does not change but the context of its application changes then only context condition should be changed. In addition, a change in context condition will change the links to its related rules.

4.2   Transaction Representation

An activity flows across several domains when a subject from one domain requests information from another domain. An example is shown in Figure 1. In the figure, LON, PERS, and INVS denote respectively the three domains "loan department", "personal banking department", and "investment department". The other two names EMP and CRTB in the figure denote respectively "the institution where the applicant is employed" and "the credit bureau". The bank policy will require the verification of the credentials of the client before approving the loan. The methods are invoked in a domain in response to requests (shown by $m_1, \ldots, m_8$) arriving from other domains. The message m_1, for example, triggers an action at the personal department. The policy for processing such requests will enforce an ordered flow of information, where a unit of information is computed by performing an *atomic* action. Hence, a transaction is composed of several atomic transactions. An atomic transaction does not involve any sub-activity and can be represented as (s, a), where a is an action performed by a subject $s \in S$.

The diagram in Figure 1, called a *work-flow* diagram, is modeled like a UML sequence diagram [6]. This differs from the notation used in work flow management systems [1]. Assuming that every action in a work-flow diagram is atomic we construct an expression equivalent to the work-flow diagram, and enforce policies for the execution of each action. The construction involves the composition constructs $\gg$ (sequential), $\|$ (parallel), $\circ$ (conjunction with no order), and $\diamond$ (priority). The expression $a \gg b$ defines the sequential composition of atomic actions a and b. That is, action a is executed, and using the result action b is executed. The parallel composition $a \| b$ is executed by simultaneous execution of actions a and b. The expression $a \circ b$ defines that action a and b should be executed by the receiver, however the order of execution is not important. The expression $a \diamond b$ defines that action a should be executed first, and if it succeeds, the action b is to be executed; otherwise, action b should be ignored and the entire action is aborted. All the constructs have the same precedence, and hence an expression

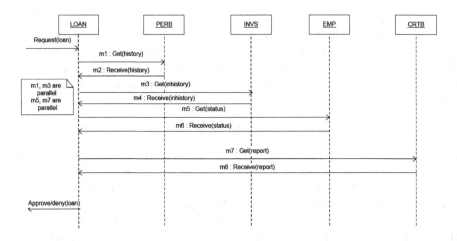

Fig. 1. Transaction - Work Flow

is evaluated from left to right. To enforce a particular order of evaluation, parenthesis may be used. Assume that each m_i in Figure 1 triggers an atomic action a_i for subject s_i. The expression constructed from the work-flow diagram is

$$((s_1, a_1) \gg (s_2, a_2)) \parallel ((s_3, a_3) \gg (s_4, a_4)) \diamond ((s_5, a_5) \gg (s_6, a_6)) \diamond ((s_7, a_7) \gg (s_8, a_8))$$

An activity requiring the collaboration of several individuals, or groups, necessarily involves a non-atomic action. We can use the same notation shown in Figure 1 for showing the work-flow arising from a non-atomic activity, except that actions in some domains at the work-flow diagram will be non-atomic. A non-atomic action at a domain gives rise to a new work-flow diagram. If this work-flow diagram includes a non-atomic action at a domain, we develop a new work-flow diagram for that action. We continue to develop work-flow diagrams recursively for each non-atomic action until all actions in a work-flow diagram are atomic. From each work-flow diagrams in which all actions are atomic we construct an expression. The expressions are composed in the reverse order of the decomposition of work-flow diagrams. From this discussion it is clear that it is sufficient to consider the secure transaction of an expression in which each action is atomic. Based on this discussion the work-flow expression, denoted wfe, corresponding to a work-flow diagram wf is defined

$$wfe ::= (s, a) \mid (wfe) \mid wfe \gg wfe \mid wfe \parallel wfe \mid wfe \circ wfe \mid wfe \diamond wfe$$

5   Secure Transaction

A work-flow wf is *secure* if in the specification wfe if the subject s in (s, a) is authorized to perform the action a, and the transaction is consistent with information flow policy. From the definition of wfe it is clear that it is sufficient to discuss security conditions for the five expressions (s, a), $(s_1, a_1) \gg (s_2, a_2)$, $(s_1, a_1) \parallel (s_2, a_2)$, $(s_1, a_1) \circ (s_2, a_2)$, and $(s_1, a_1) \diamond (s_2, a_2)$.

Security Conditions for Atomic Activity (SCA) Let (s, a) be an atomic activity. Because the activity is atomic there is no loss of generality in assuming that the subject s belongs to the domain in which the activity a arises. The subject s can be an individual, or play a role, or a member of a group.

Requester Authorization The identity of the requester who triggers action a must be proved by subject s and authorized to receive the requested service. The context c in which the request is initiated includes the credentials of the requester, in addition to those mentioned in the definition of ESC.

1. [Rules for domain d:] The set PB_s of rules in PB that s is allowed to follow in domain d is:
$$PB_s = \begin{cases} DP(s_d) & \text{if s is an individual} \\ \bigcup_{s \in g} DP(s) & \text{if s is in group g} \\ \bigcup_{x \in R} DP(x) & \text{s plays the roles R} \end{cases}$$

2. [Select the rules that are relevant for context c:] For each rule $r \in PB_s$, $r :: (U : H \Leftarrow H)$, evaluate the context condition U at context c. This is done by substituting the values in c that are appropriate for the predicates in U. If U evaluates to true at c then the rule r is relevant for context c. The set $PB'_s = \{r \in PB_s \mid r \text{ is relevant}\}$ is the set of relevant rules that s can use in context c.

3. [Remove rules not useful for the credentials:]: It is sufficient to use those rules in each of which the body of the rule is satisfied by the credential, which is part of context c. The set $PB''_s = \{r \in PB'_s \mid \text{credential satisfies } B\}$. If the set $PB''_s \neq \emptyset$, the requester is validated. However, if $PB''_s = \emptyset$ the credential cannot satisfy the body of any rule and hence the requester's identity is not established. The expression $PB @ c$ (see section 2.3) should be interpreted in this manner.

4. [Validate the requested service a:] If there exists a rule $r, r \in PB''_s$, and the head of the rule H *implies* the action a, then the request of the requester is valid; otherwise, the request is not valid.

Secure Execution If the validation is successful, the grant policy discussed in Section 2.3 is enforced.

Security Condition for Non-atomic Executions We discuss security conditions for the execution of expressions $(s_1, a_1) \gg (s_2, a_2)$, $(s_1, a_1) \parallel (s_2, a_2)$, $(s_1, a_1) \circ (s_2, a_2)$, and $(s_1, a_1) \diamond (s_2, a_2)$. These expressions respectively represent *explicit data flow*, *absence of data flow*, *implicit data flow*, and *conditional data flow*.

1. [explicit data flow] $(s_1, a_1) \gg (s_2, a_2)$: A request that triggers this compound transaction, will trigger (s_1, a_1). This being an atomic action, the security condition SCA will be applied. If action a_1 is successfully fulfilled, then subject s_1 must obey *obligations* attached to this action. An example obligation is "inform the user

if her personal information is modified". An obligation rule is independent of rules that enforce security within the system. The result of executing action a_1 must be communicated along a secure channel to subject s_2, provided the information flow policy discussed in Section 3 allows such a communication. The action (s_2, a_2) being atomic, the security condition SCA will be applied. If action a_2 is successfully fulfilled then subject s_2 must obey obligations attached to action a_2.

2. [absence of data flow] $(s_1, a_1) \parallel (s_2, a_2)$: A request that triggers this compound transaction, will trigger (s_1, a_1) and (s_2, a_2) simultaneously and independently. That is, one subject is not aware of the other subject involved in the transaction. Hence there is no information flow between s_1 and s_2. For each atomic action, the security condition SCA will be applied. Notice that the requestor who triggers this compound action will have to be authorized independently by s_1 and s_2. If action a_i is successfully fulfilled, then subject s_i must obey obligations attached to this action. It is possible that one of the actions fails while the other succeeds.

3. [implicit data flow] $(s_1, a_1) \circ (s_2, a_2)$: If $s_1 = s_2$, then this compound action is necessarily sequential. The authorization procedure is as in "explicit data flow". If $s_1 \neq s_2$, then the requester will trigger both subjects, and will have to be identified independently by both subjects. Different scenarios arise: (1) subject s_1 completes action a_1 and communicates the result to s_2; (2) subject s_1 determines that some information from s_2 is required to complete action a_1. The two other scenarios are mirror images of the above two scenarios. These scenarios are mutually exclusive, and hence only one will occur. The one that occurs, is a sequential composition, with or without data sharing. Hence, the information flow is implicit, not visible to the user. Security conditions discussed in "explicit data flow" are sufficient to be applied here.

4. [conditional data flow] $(s_1, a_1) \diamond (s_2, a_2)$: A request that triggers this compound transaction, will trigger (s_1, a_1). This being an atomic action, the security condition SCA will be applied. If action a_1 is successfully fulfilled, then subject s_1 must obey obligations attached to this action and rest of the procedure is as in sequential data flow. If (s_1, a_1) fails either because of authorization failure or the inability of internal security policy to fulfill the request, the entire transaction is abandoned.

6   Conclusion

Protecting the identity of an individual and at the same time validating the credentials submitted by an individual for services at organizational levels are important issues. An individual should exercise caution in every day life to protect the certificates that establish her identity. At the organizational level, there is a dual responsibility - ability to authenticate clients for services and protect the confidentiality of data concerning individuals. Without authentication of clients, information get stolen and benefits may reach wrong persons. Without confidentiality, personal information of individuals may be revealed violating the fundamental right of an individual to privacy. At the same time, neither of these can be administered in an extremely harsh manner: genuine people get offended when a routine identity check is strictly enforced and certain sectors may not function without getting useful information from other sectors. Balancing these apparently conflicting needs is a challenge. In this paper we have thoroughly analyzed the sources of identity threats, and investigated some solutions to thwart it. The solutions that we have put forth need to be evaluated in a practical setting, at least by simulating different scenarios. It is our intent to do that in future.

References

1. E. Bertino, E. Ferrari, V. Atluri, "A Flexible Model for the Specification and Enforcement of Role-Based Authorizations in Workflow Management Systems," In *Proceedings of the 2nd ACM Workshop on Role-Based Access Control* (RBAC-97), ACM Press, New York, 1997, pp. 6-7.
2. S. Claußand M. Köhntopp. *Identity management and its support of multilateral security.* Computer Networks, **37** (2001), 205–219.
3. N. Damianou, N. Dulay, E. Lupu, and M. Solomon. *The Ponder Policy Specification Language.* Proceedings Policy 2001: Workshop on Policies for Distributed Systems and Networks, Bristol, UK, 29–31, Jan. 2001.
4. J. DeTreville. *Binder, a logic-based security language.* Proceedings of the 2002 IEEE Symposium on Security and Privacy, IEEE Computer Society Press, May 2002, 105-113.
5. R. Ortalo. *A Flexible Method for Information System Security Policy Specification.* Proceedings of 5th European Symposium on Research in Computer Security, 1998. Louvain-la-Neuve, Belgium, Springer-Verlag.
6. J. Rumbaugh, et al: The Unified Modeling Language Reference Manual, Addison-Wesley.
7. Kaiyu Wan, Vasu Alagar. *Security Contexts in Autonomic Computing Systems.* In *Proceedings of Proceedings of 2006 International Conference on Computational Intelligence and Security (CIS2006)*, November 03-06, 2006, Guangzhou, PRC, page 1523-1527. (also to appear in Lecture Notes in Artificial Intelligence)
8. Fighting Back Against Identity Theft - U.S. Federal Trade Commission. www.ftc.gov/bcp/edu/microsites/idtheft/
9. Identity Theft: What is it and What you can do about it?, Office of the Privacy Commissioner of Canada, www.privcom.gc.ca/fs-fi/02_05_d_10_e.asp/
10. European Conference "Maintaining the integrity of identities and payments: Two challenges for fraud prevention". ec.europa.eu/justice_home/news/information_dossiers/conference_integrity/index_en.htm/

Automated Privacy Audits to Complement the Notion of Control for Identity Management

Rafael Accorsi

Department of Telematics
Albert-Ludwigs-Universität Freiburg, Germany
`accorsi@iig.uni-freiburg.de`

Abstract. Identity management systems are indispensable in modern networked computing, as they equip data providers with key techniques to avoid the imminent privacy threats intrinsic to such environments. Their rationale is to convey data providers with a sense of *control* over the disclosure and usage of personal data to varying degree, so that they can take an active role in protecting their privacy. However, we purport the thesis that a holistic sense of control includes not only the *regulation* of disclosure, as identity management techniques currently do, but must equivalently comprise the *supervision* of compliance, i.e. credible evidence that data consumers behave according to the policies previously agreed upon. Despite its relevance, supervision has so far not been possible. We introduce the concept of *privacy evidence* and present the necessary technical building blocks to realise it in dynamic systems.

1 Introduction

In a technological setting where some even prophesy the death of privacy [5], the need for approaches to mediate and legislate for the collection of personal attributes and their usage is increasingly gaining in momentum and relevance. While such an investigation involves interdisciplinary efforts, we focus on the technical aspects. In this context, identity management systems (henceforth IMS) play an essential role in circumventing the privacy threats inherent to the deployment of information technology. They allow data providers to selectively disclose attributes to data consumers, possibly enabling data providers to formulate policies under which collected attributes can or cannot be employed.

The rationale of IMS is to convey a sense of control to data providers, where the "control" stands for the *regulation* of attribute disclosure. However, data providers today obtain no indication as to whether data consumers actually behave according to the policies agreed upon. Put other way, data providers are left with a number of privacy promises or expectations, but obtain no creditable evidence that their policies have been adhered to. Thus, this setting clearly fails to reproduce the established understanding of control individuals have in mind, in which control comprises not only the regulation of a set of activities, but also the *supervision* that this set of activities indeed takes place as expected. As a result of lacking supervision, data consumers often fear that their personal attributes could be (illegally) shared with third parties or used for purposes other than those stated [12].

Please use the following format when citing this chapter:

Accorsi, R., 2008, in IFIP International Federation for Information Processing, Volume 261; *Policies and Research in Identity Management*; Eds. E. de Leeuw, Fischer-Hübner, S., Tseng, J., Borking, J.; (Boston: Springer), pp. 39–48.

We close this gap by investigating the technical building blocks necessary to realise supervision in dynamic systems, i.e. open and adaptive systems based on ubiquitous computing technologies [9]. Addressing supervision requires a conceptional change, though. Traditional IMS build on observability, unlinkability and unidentifiability and therefore use a number of techniques, such as pseudonyms and partial identities over anonymous communication channels. In addition to this, recent IMS allow data providers to formulate policies and stick them to data, a concept called to as "sticky policies" [4]. (We refer to [10] for a comprehensive survey on techniques for IMS.) Thus, current techniques aim at an *a priori*, preventive protection of privacy. In contrast, when investigating supervision we found ourselves in an *a posteriori* setting where techniques to verify the compliance with privacy policies are needed.

To realise this, we employ the concept of *privacy evidence* [12]. Its rationale is to make the behaviour of the data consumer regarding data collection and enforcement of privacy policies evident to data providers. Intuitively, a privacy evidence is a record consisting, on the one hand, of all the information collected from and related to a particular data provider – a so-called *log view* – and, on the other hand, the result of an automated audit of this log view based on the policies of the data provider. Together, these pieces of information build the basis for supervision and thereby pave the way for a holistic realisation of control.

The thesis we purport is that investigation towards a holistic realisation of control for informational self-determination in IMS is indispensable. Due to the improved transparency inherent to privacy evidence, such realisation of control has the chance to increase the confidence placed on the data consumers and even foster the willingness to disclose personal attributes, which is an essential factor for the acceptance of dynamic system in general and for the deployment of personalised services [13] in particular. Eventually, both data providers and data consumers could equally profit from such an extended notion of control.

This paper is structured as follows. In §2, we present the technical setting underlying our approach and the main building blocks necessary to realise the concept of privacy evidence. These building blocks are then described sequentially: in §3, we introduce a language for the expression of privacy policies; in §4, log views based on a secure logging service are presented; and in §5, we describe our approach to auditing log views based on the stated privacy policies. We discuss our work and provide perspectives for further work in §6.

2   Technical Setting and Building Blocks

The realisation of privacy evidence anticipates the steps depicted in Fig. 1. In (1), a data provider A formulates a policy P_A and communicates it to the data consumer. Since we consider dynamic systems with implicit interactions, we assume that policies are communicated before joining the system. (Implicit interactions take place without the awareness of the data provider.) When interacting with the system, a number of events are recorded as entries in log files (2). In fact, we assume that *every* event is recorded, so that log files offer a complete digital representation of the activity in a dynamic system. At some point in time the data consumer may retrieve the log view S_A containing all

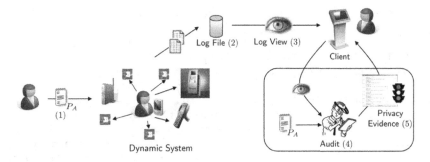

Fig. 1. The workflow for privacy evidence.

the log entries related to A (3). A can then visualise the collected data and start a third-party automated audit process (4) to check whether the policies P_A have been adhered to, thereby generating the corresponding privacy evidence (5).

To realise privacy evidence, the following central technical building blocks are essential: a *policy language* for the expression of privacy preferences in dynamic systems; *log views* to allow the visualisation of recording activity; a *secure logging* to ensure the authenticity of recorded data, in particular to improve the credibility of log views; and an *automated audit* process for checking the adherence to policies. In the forthcoming sections, we describe the work towards the realisation of privacy evidence.

Assumptions. In our work, we consider the following assumptions. First, *every* event happening in the system, as well as every access to collected data is recorded as an event in a log file. Second, on interacting with the system, data providers are identified while the events they are involved in are recorded. That is, the entries in the log file are always related to a data provider. Third, while the system is dynamic in that it adapts itself to the data providers' preferences, it is static regarding the data collection possibilities. Technically, this means that the ontology describing the system does not change over time and, hence, the policies of data providers do not become obsolete. Although these assumptions do not hold in general, they hold for some scenarios, as the one we consider in §6.

3   A Policy Language for Dynamic Systems

A policy language allows data providers to specify a set of rules, i.e. a policy to regulate the access to their attributes, whereas execution monitors on the data consumers' side enforce these rules and record the authorisation decisions for further inspection. However, in dynamic systems the sole expression of access rights is not enough. Policies for dynamic systems should also allow data providers to express which attributes may or may not be collected. The policy language we propose therefore builds on two notions: *access* and *collection*. In contexts where the distinction between these notions is irrelevant, we simply refer to them as an *act*.

We enrich atomic acts with conditions for *usage control*. Usage control extends traditional access control techniques by allowing data providers to specify *provisions*

```
1.  <Policy>      := (<Rule>) | (<Rule>), <Policy>
2.  <Rule>        := <Col_Ctrl> | <Col_Ctrl>, if (<Cond>) |
3.                   <Acc_Ctrl> | <Acc_Ctrl>, if (<Cond>)
4.  <Col_Ctrl>    := <Perm>, <Subj>, <Obj>, <Event>
5.  <Acc_Ctrl>    := <Perm>, <Subj>, <Obj>, <Right>
6.  <Cond>        := <Atom_Cond> | <Atom_Cond> && <Cond>
7.  <Atom_Cond>   := <Provision> | <Obligation>
8.  <Provision>   := role <Op> <Role> | purpose <Op> <Purpose> |
9.                   <DataField> <Op> <Value>
10. <Obligation>  := delete <DataField> <Temp_mod> [<Sanction>] |
11.                  notify <DataProvider> <Temp_mod> [<Sanction>]
12. <Perm>        := allow | deny
13. <Right>       := read | write | exec <Cmd>
14. <Temp_mod>    := immediately | within <Nat_Number> days
15. <Sanction>    := otherwise <String>
16. <Op>          := > | < | >= | <= | == | !=
```

Fig. 2. Policy language for dynamic systems.

and *obligations* [11]. Intuitively, provisions express the conditions that must be fulfilled in order to grant or deny an act [7]. For example, access to the profile of data provider A is granted only for accounting purposes. Obligations express events that must occur once an act is granted or denied. For example, data provider A wants to be notified whenever the collection of attributes via RFID readers take place.

Figure 2 depicts the core definition of our policy language in BNF-notation. Intuitively, the policy of a data provider A is a finite set of rules $P_A = \{r_1, \ldots, r_n\}$ (Line 1), each of which can stand for a (conditional) act, i.e. collection or access regulation (Lines 2 and 3). When formulating a collection rule, A stipulates whether a certain subject is able to collect an attribute and/or event (Line 4). The same applies for the formulation of access rules (Line 5). In both cases, the wildcard $\star$ can be used to represent a whole class of, e.g., subjects or attributes. Conditions can include provisions and obligations (Line 7): provisions regard the role a subject takes, as well as the purpose of the access or collection and the value of collected data fields serving as guards (Lines 8 and 9); obligations encompass the deletion of some attribute within a certain timeframe and the notification of individuals (Lines 10 and 11). Obligations may or may well not include sanctions that hold in case a particular obligation is not fulfilled (Line 15).

The actual value of terminals, such as Obj and Subj are application-dependent and omitted here for simplicity. (To this end, we have defined data models corresponding to our scenario.) To illustrate how formulated rules appear and exemplify their expressive power, in Fig. 3 we consider two rules for the data provider A. Rule r_1, stipulates that A grants read access to his attributes provided the accessing subject adopts the role "Marketing", the purpose is personalised service and the accessed attribute is deleted within 30 days. In the case of non-adherence, a compensation of \$100 is due. Rule r_2 prohibits the collection of data by RFID-readers.

```
r₁ := ( allow, *, *, read,
        if ( role == Marketing &&
             purpose == PersService &&
             delete * within 30 days otherwise Fine=$100$ ))
r₂ := ( deny, RFID-Reader, *, * )
```

Fig. 3. Examples of policy rules.

4   Secure Logging and Log Views

Log data is a central source of information in computer systems. In contrast to other rather "static" files, such as text documents or spreadsheets, log files allow one to reconstruct the dynamics of a system, i.e. the course of events that led to some particular state. Hence, log files are a central source of information for audits. However, to be useful and credible, log data must be authentic, i.e. it must fulfil the following properties [1]:

- *Integrity* states that log data faithfully reflects the state of the devices, i.e., the log data is accurate (entries have not been modified), complete (entries have not been deleted), and compact (entries have not been illegally added to the log file). Thus, log data is not modified, deleted, or appended during the transmission to and storage at the collector.
- *Confidentiality* states that log entries cannot be stored in clear-text, for such log data can be easily accessed to duplicated.

The authenticity properties of log data must be realised with cryptographic techniques which account for *tamper evidence*, i.e., attempts to illicitly manipulate log data are detectable to a verifier, and *forward integrity*, i.e. log data contains sufficient information to confirm or rebuke allegations of log data modification before the moment of the compromise. (Put another way, forward integrity states that if an attacker succeeds in breaking in at time t, log data stored before t cannot be compromised.)

Based on [1], we present below the basis of a secure logging service. There are two kinds of actors in a logging setting: the *devices* sense the environment and communicate changes therein in the form of events to a *collector*, whose responsibility is to sequentially record these events. Assuming that the communication between devices and collectors cannot be manipulated, here we focus on the collector and the corresponding mechanisms to ensure the authenticity of recorded data.

In our approach, log data is secured when recording the entry associated to an event and not as a separate process. Each log entry E_j is (symmetrically) encrypted with an evolving cryptographic key K_j obtained from a secret master key A_j and an index field W_j. (The latter is used to describe the data provider to which the entry refers.) A hash chain Y associates the previous entry E_{j-1} and the current. This procedure is depicted in Fig. 4, where the numbers correspond to:

1. $A_j = Hash(A_{j-1})$ denotes the authentication key of the jth log entry. The confidentiality of this information is essential as it is used to encrypt log entries. Thus, we

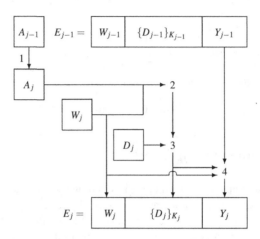

Fig. 4. Adding an entry to the log file.

assume that the computation of the new value irretrievably overwrites the previous value.

2. $K_j = Hash(W_j, A_j)$ is the cryptographic key with which the jth log entry is encrypted. This key is based on the index W_j, so that only corresponding data providers gain access to the entry.

3. $\{D_j\}_{K_j}$ is the encrypted log entry D_j.

4. $Y_j = Hash(Y_{j-1}, \{D_j\}_{K_j}, W_j)$ is the jth value of the hash chain. Each link of the hash chain is based on the corresponding encrypted value of the log data.

The generated log entry, denoted $E_j = W_j, \{D_j\}_{K_j}, Y_j$, consists of the index W_j, the encrypted log entry $\{D_j\}_{K_j}$, and the hash chain value Y_j.

4.1 Log Views and their Generation

A central concept to allow supervision is to furnish data providers with timestamped information regarding *which* attributes have been collected, *who* has had access to them and *how* collected attributes have been used. In our approach, these pieces of information are compiled into a *log view* [12], a concept bearing similarity with its homonymous counterpart in the field of databases.

Log views are individualised audit trails consisting of factual data (performed transactions, collected attributes, etc.) and monitored data (access and usage information) about a particular data provider, as well as meta data – in the form of a digital signature – about the generating data consumer and the integrity of a view. Figure 5 illustrates a part of log view of a data provider referred to as "bernauer".

As for the generation of log views, to retrieve a log view S_A the data provider A employs a trusted device (e.g. a home computer or a terminal dedicated to this purpose) to authenticate himself to the data consumer, who then starts a query over (possibly distributed) log files. Intuitively, the index of each entry is checked against the authenticated data provider. If they match and the entry passes an integrity check (based on

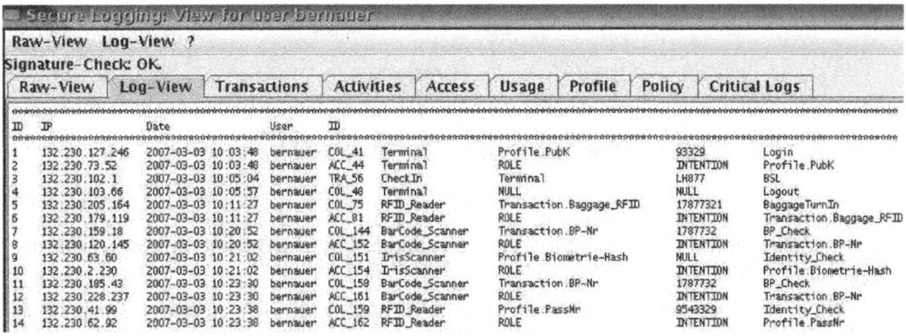
Secure Logging: View for user bernauer
Raw-View Log-View ?
Signature-Check: OK.
Raw-View | Log-View | Transactions | Activities | Access | Usage | Profile | Policy | Critical Logs

ID	IP	Date	User	ID				
1	132.230.127.246	2007-03-03 10:03:48	bernauer	COL_41	Terminal	Profile.PubK	93329	Login
2	132.230.73.52	2007-03-03 10:03:48	bernauer	ACC_44	Terminal	ROLE	INTENTION	Profile.PubK
3	132.230.102.1	2007-03-03 10:05:04	bernauer	TRA_56	CheckIn	Terminal	LH877	BSL
4	132.230.103.66	2007-03-03 10:05:57	bernauer	COL_48	Terminal	NULL	NULL	Logout
5	132.230.205.164	2007-03-03 10:11:27	bernauer	COL_75	RFID_Reader	Transaction.Baggage_RFID	17877321	BaggageTurnIn
6	132.230.179.119	2007-03-03 10:11:27	bernauer	ACC_81	RFID_Reader	ROLE	INTENTION	Transaction.Baggage_RFID
7	132.230.159.18	2007-03-03 10:20:52	bernauer	COL_144	BarCode_Scanner	Transaction.BP-Nr	1787732	BP_Check
8	132.230.120.145	2007-03-03 10:20:52	bernauer	ACC_152	BarCode_Scanner	ROLE	INTENTION	Transaction.BP-Nr
9	132.230.63.60	2007-03-03 10:21:02	bernauer	COL_151	IrisScanner	Profile.Biometrie-Hash	NULL	Identity_Check
10	132.230.2.230	2007-03-03 10:21:02	bernauer	ACC_154	IrisScanner	ROLE	INTENTION	Profile.Biometrie-Hash
11	132.230.185.43	2007-03-03 10:23:30	bernauer	COL_158	BarCode_Scanner	Transaction.BP-Nr	1787732	BP_Check
12	132.230.228.237	2007-03-03 10:23:30	bernauer	ACC_161	BarCode_Scanner	ROLE	INTENTION	Transaction.BP-Nr
13	132.230.41.99	2007-03-03 10:23:38	bernauer	COL_159	RFID_Reader	Profile.PassNr	9543329	Identity_Check
14	132.230.62.92	2007-03-03 10:23:38	bernauer	ACC_162	RFID_Reader	ROLE	INTENTION	Profile.PassNr

Fig. 5. Part of a log view for data provider `bernauer`.

the hash chain), then the content of the entry is decrypted and added to the log view of A. When all the entries are queried, the resultant view is signed and sent back to the inquiring data provider.

5 Automated Audits and Digital Privacy Evidence

Log views would, at least in theory, suffice to realise the holistic sense of control we argue for in this manuscript: data providers could browse through their log views and check whether their privacy policies have been adhered to or not. However, this is more intricate than it seems. Log views can easily include thousands of entries and their interrelationships are often hard to comprehend and reconstruct, regardless of how much effort we put into improving their readability.

We develop an approach to audit log views parameterised by the policies of data providers. Intuitively, given a policy $P := \{r_1, \ldots, r_n\}$ and a log view S, we define a transformation v that takes P and returns the set of rules $V_P = \{v_1, \ldots, v_n\}$ such that each $v_i \in V$ denotes the violation of the corresponding rule r_i. To illustrate this, consider the rule r_2 in Fig. 3. By applying the transformation v, the following violation is generated:

v_2 := `( allow, RFID-Reader, *, * ).`

This denotes that the collection of attributes through RFID readers is allowed, thereby contradicting the original desire of the data provider.

With V_P at hand, we then search for violations in the log view of the corresponding data provider. To this end, we define the pinpoint relation $\triangleright$ between views and the set of violations V_P such that $S \triangleright v_i$ if v_i can be pinpointed, i.e. detected, in S. If there is a $v_i \in V_P$ such that $S \triangleright v_i$, then there is an execution of the system that violates r_i and, in consequence, the policy P. In contrast, if there is no such v_i, such that $S \triangleright v_i$, then a violation of P can be ruled out. Technical details are found in [2].

We employ a semaphore notation to make the result of audit evident to the pertinent data provider. In this case, red obviously stands for a violation of some rule, while green denotes the compliance with a policy. An amber semaphore indicates that some obligation-based rule could not be pinpointed and therefore stands for a warning. Such

Fig. 6. Condition leading to an amber semaphore

a warning is triggered whenever a log view S is audited before the deadline of a pending obligation, as illustrated in Fig. 6.

A log view, together with the corresponding audit analysis, constitutes a privacy evidence. In the case of a violation, an individual may click over the semaphore and obtain details on which rules have been violated as well as the entries that led to this result. A similar procedure can be carried out when the semaphore shows amber.

6   Discussion and Perspectives

Taking stock, in this manuscript we purport the thesis that a holistic notion of control for IMS encompasses not only the regulation of communicated (respectively, collected) attributes, but also the supervision of adherence to stated policies. While this understanding of control as regulation and (at least the option of) supervision is prevalent in the common language, to our knowledge it has not been considered in the context of IMS. We firmly believe that the investigation of approaches to realise such forms of control is the next milestone towards the development of IMS to cope with the privacy challenges of dynamic systems.

We see various advantages arising from a holistic notion of control. Today, individuals tend to have doubt than confidence that computing systems behave according to privacy policies. In consequence, individuals aware of the imminent privacy threats are reluctant to use technologies, even in cases where this would be advantageous. The use of tools supporting the regulation and supervision introduced in this manuscript offer a unique chance to revert these figures. For individuals can only feel confident when a certain level of transparency and assurance is at hand; this is achieved by means of privacy evidence.

We currently test this approach within an airport as those proposed by the IATA. The idea is to employ several ubiquitous computing technologies to automate the check-in of passengers. Basic technologies include the replacement of traditional boarding passes with 2D barcode boarding passes that could even be printed at home and the replacement of luggage tags with RFID tags. Several airlines plan to extend the vision further and include biometric identification and other communication media, e.g. mobile phones and PDAs. In such a setting, the assumptions we made in §2 are realistic.

The ideas presented here open up several interesting perspectives for further research into the subject. Below, we elaborate on some of them. First, by relaxing the assumptions made above, we are left with the fact that log entries may fail to refer to a data provider and the question is how to decide whether an "unknown" entry refers to a particular data provider or not. This is a relevant question, as data consumers could intentionally hide relevant entries from the log view and thereby influence the result of the audit. To tackle this problem, techniques for IT forensics, possibly in combination with the methods for data mining, may be needed.

Second, the term privacy evidence has an implicit legal connotation, one we knowingly do not explore in this manuscript. While in our approach we use trusted sandboxes [3, 6] to attest the existence of the corresponding logging and log view generation algorithms, we are aware that this is not enough for judicial evidence. (We recall that the audit is performed on a trusted device and, hence, does not pose a problem.) To transform privacy evidence in legally acceptable evidence with corresponding probative force, the notion of chain-of-custody [8] for evidence, for instance, should be investigated in greater detail.

Finally, the approach we propose does not exclude traditional IMS techniques. On the contrary, it *complements* them. It would thus be interesting to see more case studies using our techniques, as well as other developments, for supervision. We believe this will substantiate the importance of supervision as a distinguishing factor for future IMS and privacy-aware (dynamic) systems.

References

1. R. Accorsi. On the relationship of privacy and secure remote logging in dynamic systems. In S. Fischer-Hübner, K. Rannemberg, L. Yngström, and S. Lindskog, editors, *Proceedings of the 21st IFIP TC-11 International Security Conference: Security and Privacy in Dynamic Environments*, volume 201 of *International Federation for Information Processing*, pages 329–339. Springer-Verlag, 2006.
2. R. Accorsi and M. Bernauer. On privacy evidence for UbiComp environments – Broadening the notion of control to improve user acceptance. In A. Bajart, H. Muller, and T. Strang, editors, *Proceedings of the 5th Workshop on Privacy in UbiComp*, pages 433–438, 2007.
3. R. Accorsi and A. Hohl. Delegating secure logging in pervasive computing systems. In J. Clark, R. Paige, F. Pollack, and P. Brooke, editors, *Proceedings of the 3rd International Conference on Security in Pervasive Computing*, volume 3934 of *Lecture Notes in Computer Science*, pages 58–72. Springer Verlag, 2006.
4. M. Casassa-Mont, S. Pearson, and P. Bramhall. Towards accountable management of privacy and identity. In E. Snekkenes and D. Gollmann, editors, *Proceedings of the European Symposium on Research in Computer Security*, volume 2808 of *Lecture Notes in Computer Science*, pages 146–161. Springer-Verlag, 2003.
5. M. Froomkin. The death of privacy? *Stanford Law Review*, 52(5):1461–1543, May 2000.
6. A. Hohl. *Traceable Processing of Personal Data in Remote Services Using TCG*. PhD thesis, University of Freiburg, 2006.
7. S. Jajodia, M. Kudo, and V. Subrahmanian. Provisional authorizations. In A. Ghosh, editor, *E-Commerce Security and Privacy*, pages 133–159. Kluwer Academic Publishers, 2001.
8. E. Kenneally. Digital logs – Proof matters. *Digital Investigation*, 1(2):94–101, June 2004.
9. G. Müller. Privacy and security in highly dynamic systems. *Communications of the ACM*, 49(9):28–31, September 2006.
10. A. Pfitzmann. Multilateral security: Enabling technologies and their evaluation. In G. Müller, editor, *Proceedings of the International Conference on Emerging Trends in Information and Communication Security*, volume 3995 of *Lecture Notes in Computer Science*, pages 1–13. Springer-Verlag, 2006.
11. A. Pretschner, M. Hilty, and D. Basin. Distributed usage control. *Communications of the ACM*, 49(9):39–44, September 2006.

12. S. Sackmann, J. Strüker, and R. Accorsi. Personalization in privacy-aware highly dynamic systems. *Communications of the ACM*, 49(9):32–38, September 2006.
13. J. Strüker. Der gläserne Kunde im Supermarkt der Zukunft. *Wirtschaftsinformatik*, 49(1):59–62, January 2007.

Privacy Enhancing Technologies

Privacy and trust in the Information Society

Dirk van Rooy

European Commission, DG Information Society and Media

Disclaimer: Any views or opinions presented are not necessarily those of the European Commission and remain the sole responsibility of the author.

Extended synopsis

The Directorate-General Information Society and Media, part of the European Commission, supports the development and use of information and communication technologies (ICT) for the benefit of all citizens and for underpinning European competitiveness and growth. Its objective is to stimulate the continued development of an all-inclusive information society, and the assurance of trust and security is pivotal to this development. Security and privacy protection are moving targets, and bringing trust into the networked society is an open-ended, permanent and multi-stakeholder endeavour..

With the daily emergence of new personalised services, we face a permanently changing threat landscape. The ICT Programme managed by DG INFSO includes key research activities supporting the development of identity management and privacy enhancing technologies to keep abreast of these mutating challenges. However, technology alone is not enough; it has to go hand in hand with other measures, including legislation and policy. Competitive markets and business opportunities should lead to a strong business drive, and last, but certainly not least, there needs to be informed and responsible user behaviour and strong well-informed user demand.

To address the above challenges, the European Union has established a well structured set of measures, including a comprehensive regulatory baseline and an ambitious research programme to stimulate technology development and uptake. These three activities – regulation, research and the promotion of wider use – form the pillars for the creation and promotion of a competitive, inclusive and trustworthy European information society and knowledge economy.

The conference of today, IDMAN 2007, offers a platform for exchanging views on the pivotal role that identity management technologies play in this context, and how these technologies can be used to enhance and protect privacy in the information society. Such initiatives are important to uncover future requirements for research and technological development in this area. The outcome of such exchanges adds to the technology pillar of providing a more secure, trustworthy and inclusive information society in the future.

The knowledge society under creation is a great step forward for mankind. It enables people to use information wherever and whenever they need it, adapted to their personal interests. Every day more and more people, organisations and devices

Please use the following format when citing this chapter:

van Rooy, D., 2008, in IFIP International Federation for Information Processing, Volume 261; *Policies and Research in Identity Management*; Eds. E. de Leeuw, Fischer-Hübner, S., Tseng, J., Borking, J.; (Boston: Springer), pp. 51–53.

get connected to the Internet. They bring more linkable information and business, and more communication. The trust and confidence of end-users in ICT services are crucial in order for this evolving information society to remain successful. Employees connect remotely to their organisation. Consumers leave personal information almost everywhere, and these data are stored – sometimes for a life-time – on interconnected systems everywhere. Collaborative work beyond company and organisational boundaries, across the globe, is becoming a daily thing.

Identity management with proper privacy protection and user empowerment is of key importance for creating the necessary trust for a continued development of the digital society. On May 2nd, 2007, the Commission adopted a policy on Promoting Data Protection by Privacy Enhancing Technologies (PETs), part of a bouquet of regulatory and policy initiatives in the domain of ensuring a trustworthy all-inclusive knowledge society. This policy underlines that privacy is a fundamental right implemented in EU directives and Member States' legislation. However, this might be insufficient when personal data are disseminated worldwide, and when – in sync with the development of new ICT services – new risks arise. The PETs Communication calls for follow-up actions, including stepping up research and development, promoting the use of PETs by data controllers, standardization, and raising consumer awareness to facilitate informed choice making. The PETs information pack is available at ec.europa.eu/information_society/activities/privtech.

Other initiatives aiming at increasing security in the networked society include the adoption of a strategy for a secure information society (2006). The essential elements of this European strategy are dialogue, partnership and empowerment amongst the key stakeholders. In 2006 the Commission adopted a policy on fighting spam, spyware and malicious software. Another example is RFID, a technology that offers great economic potential, but at the same time is an attractive target for attackers and potentially a risk to privacy. The Commission has organised a broad consultation and adopted a policy that puts particular emphasis on security and privacy. As we do not only need protection and prevention, but also deterrence, the Commission adopted in 2007 a policy on cybercrime.

It is clear that most technology can be used in different ways, for example by states that want to control and supervise their people. But let us not only look at possible abuse of information by states, but also by private data controllers, for example companies collecting and using identity and profiling data for their own profit, without much regard for privacy and the personal sphere. ICT systems do not need to store personal data attributes for running application services together with the identity data to which the attributes belong. The linkage of identity data with profiling and other personal data attributes can be controlled by the user. There is a need for ID management standards at the meta level that enable controlled separation from application management, and the principles of minimum transfer of identifiable data should be implemented.

On the research side the EU has been funding research and development in the area of ICT trust and security for many years. As part of the 6th RTD Framework Programme (2002-2006) about 35 projects centred in this area were funded, amounting to about €145 million funding contribution. We are currently in the initial phase of launching new projects under the ICT Programme of FP7 (2007-2013). Further information can be found at: http://cordis.europa.eu/fp7/ict/security.

The evolving knowledge society is a major step forward for mankind. It enables people to use information wherever and whenever they need it, adapted to their personal interests. We should ensure that this new society is a society for all, a society built on confidence and trust.

Biometrics

Biometric Encryption: Technology for Strong Authentication, Security and Privacy

Ann Cavoukian, Alex Stoianov and Fred Carter

Office of the Information and Privacy Commissioner, Toronto, Ontario, Canada
{commissioner, Alex.Stoianov, Fred.Carter}@ipc.on.ca

Abstract. This paper looks at privacy-enhanced uses of biometrics, with a particular focus on the privacy and security advantages of Biometric Encryption (BE). It considers the merits of Biometric Encryption for verifying identity, protecting privacy, and ensuring security. In doing so, it argues that BE technologies can help to overcome the prevailing "zero-sum" mentality, which posits that adding privacy to identification and information systems will necessarily weaken security and functionality. It explains how and why BE technology promises a "win-win" scenario for all stakeholders.

1 Biometrics and Privacy

During the past decade we have witnessed a rapid evolution and maturation of biometric (and other) information technologies. Biometric technologies are now being deployed in a wide range of public and private sector uses and applications, including: physical and logical access controls, attendance recording, payment systems, crime and fraud prevention/detection, and border security controls.

Biometric technologies are now reaching an important threshold in terms of general awareness, acceptance and widespread use.

Biometric technologies promise many benefits, including stronger user authentication, greater user convenience, and improved security and operational efficiencies.

Biometric technologies are not, however, without their challenges and their risks. These include some important technological challenges (such as accuracy, reliability, data security, user acceptance, cost, and interoperability), as well as challenges associated with ensuring effective privacy protections.

Of particular concern when we talk about biometrics is the concept of informational privacy, referring generally to an individual's *personal* control over the collection, use and disclosure of recorded information about them, as well as to an organization's responsibility for data protection and the safeguarding of personally identifiable information (PII), in its custody or control.

A lack of informational privacy can have profound negative impacts on user confidence, trust, and the usage of a given information technology, specific application or deployment, or even an entire industry.

Please use the following format when citing this chapter:

Cavoukian, A., Stoianov, A. and Carter, F., 2008, in IFIP International Federation for Information Processing, Volume 261; *Policies and Research in Identity Management*; Eds. E. de Leeuw, Fischer-Hübner, S., Tseng, J., Borking, J.; (Boston: Springer), pp. 57–77.

The privacy concerns associated with biometric technologies and the collection, use, and retention of biometric data have been extensively documented[i], and include:

- unauthorized secondary uses of biometric data (function creep);
- expanded surveillance tracking, profiling, and potential discrimination;
- data misuse (data breach, identity fraud and theft);
- negative personal impacts of false matches, non-matches, system errors and failures;
- diminished oversight, accountability, and openness of biometric data systems;
- absence of individual knowledge and consent; loss of personal control.

Many responses to these privacy concerns and risks have been proposed, including strengthening legal and regulatory oversight mechanisms, developing and operationalizing clear data usage policies, and improving education and awareness efforts. The general intent of these approaches is to minimize identified risks to acceptable levels and to encourage user confidence.

Some critics have gone further to advocate more structural approaches to protecting privacy in biometric systems, for example, by limiting the design and operation of biometric technologies to authentication (1:1) only, rather than identification (1:n) purposes[ii].

International data protection commissioners, for example, have consistently argued against creating large, centralized databases of biometric data[iii]. They have also encouraged the development and use of privacy-enhancing technologies (PETs) that express internationally accepted fair information principles directly into the information system. PETs enable individuals to manage their own personally identifiable information (PII) and minimize privacy risks at an earlier, more granular level.[iv] They do this by:

- actively engaging the individual in managing and controlling their own PII (e.g., consent, accuracy, access, challenging compliance);
- minimizing the collection, use, disclosure and retention of PII by others (e.g., limiting purposes, collection, use, retention, etc.); and
- enhancing data security (e.g., safeguards).[v]

Some critics suggest that deploying PETs would hinder the objectives and functions of biometric-enabled information systems and applications. This is based on the common assumption, belief or argument that individual privacy must necessarily be sacrificed to broader societal, programmatic and operational needs, for example, accountability and security.

In our view, engineering privacy into (biometric) information systems is not only desirable and possible, but can also be accomplished in a manner that achieves positive-sum results for all stakeholders. Biometric Encryption (BE) technologies – the particular PETs that we will explore here in detail – are a good example of how privacy and security can both be increased in a positive-sum model.

BE is, in our view, worthy of consideration for a wide range of private and public sector uses, where user confidence and trust are critical success factors.

2   Security Vulnerabilities of a Biometric System

Biometric systems, especially those based on one-to-one authentication, are vulnerable to potential attacks.[vi] Vulnerabilities include:

- **Spoofing**. It has been demonstrated that a biometric system sometimes can be fooled by applying fake fingerprints, face or iris image, etc.
- **Replay attacks**, e.g. circumventing the sensor by injecting a recorded image in the system input, which is much easier than attacking the sensor.
- **Substitution attack**: The biometric template must be stored to allow user verification. If an attacker gets access to the storage, either locally or remotely, he can overwrite the legitimate user's template with his/her own – in essence, stealing their identity.
- **Tampering**: Feature sets on verification or in the templates can be modified in order to obtain a high verification score, no matter which image is presented to the system, or, alternatively, to bring the system down by making the score low for legitimate users.
- **Masquerade attack**. It was demonstrated[vii, viii] that a digital "artefact" image can be created from a fingerprint template, so that this artefact, if submitted to the system, will produce a match. The artefact may not even resemble the original image. This attack poses a real threat to the remote authentication systems (e.g. via the Web), since an attacker does not even have to bother to acquire a genuine biometric sample. All he needs is just to gain an access to the templates stored on a remote server.
- **Trojan horse attacks**: Some parts of the system, such as a matcher, can be replaced by a Trojan horse program that always outputs high verification scores.
- **Overriding Yes/No response**. An inherent flaw of existing biometric systems is that the output of the system is always a binary Yes/No (i.e., match/no match) response. In other words, there is a fundamental disconnect between the biometric and applications, which makes the system open to potential attacks. For example, if an attacker were able to interject a false Yes response at a proper point of the communication between the biometrics and the application, he could pose as a legitimate user to any of the applications, thus bypassing the biometric part.
- **Insufficient accuracy** of many commercial biometric systems, both in terms of False Rejection Rate (FRR) and False Acceptance Rate (FAR). High FRR causes inconvenience for legitimate users and prompts the system administrator to lower a verification threshold. This inevitably gives rise to FAR, which, in turn, lowers the security level of the system.

The privacy and security issues of a biometric system outlined in this section are illustrated in Fig. 1 below:

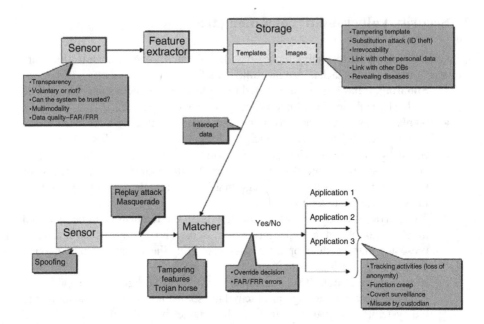

Fig. 1. Privacy and security issues in a biometric system

The enrolment part of any conventional biometric system consists of at least three blocks: a biometric sensor which acquires an image, a feature extractor that creates a biometric template, and storage for the templates, or images, or both. The storage can be either a database or a distributed medium.

The verification or identification part contains (at a minimum) a sensor to acquire a new image sample, and a matcher, which compares the image with the previously enrolled template(s) received from the storage. The output of the matcher is a Yes/No (i.e., match/no match) response that may go to the variety of applications.

A user of the system faces several privacy issues immediately at enrolment:

- Transparency, i.e., if the purpose of the system is clear to the user;
- If the enrolment is voluntary, and what are the consequences of not getting enrolled (for a variety of reasons);
- If the system can be trusted, i.e., if the personal data are adequately protected;
- Quality of biometric data: poor quality may lead to higher FRR and FAR. While FAR increases security risks for the system, a false rejection often causes some follow-up procedures which can be privacy-invasive to the individual.

3   Biometrics and Cryptography

Conventional cryptography uses encryption keys, which are just long bit strings, usually 128 bits or more. These keys – which can be symmetric, public, or private— are an essential part of any cryptosystem, for example, Public Key Infrastructure

(PKI). A person cannot memorize such a long random key, so the key is generated, using several steps, from a password or a PIN that can be memorized. The password management is the weakest point of any cryptosystem, as the password can be guessed, found with a brute force search, or stolen by an attacker.

Biometrics, on the other hand, are unique characteristics that are always there. Can they be used as a cryptographic key? Unfortunately, the answer is negative: biometric images or templates are variable by nature, which means that each new biometric sample is different. And conventional cryptography cannot tolerate a single bit error.

A biometric system always produces a Yes/No response, which is essentially one bit of information. Therefore, an obvious role for biometrics in the conventional cryptosystem is password management, as mentioned by Bruce Schneier[ix]. Upon receiving Yes response, the system unlocks a password or a key. The key must be stored in a secure location (so called "trusted" device). This scheme is still prone to the security vulnerabilities noted in Fig. 1, however, since the biometric system and the password are connected via one bit only.

Biometric templates or images stored in a database can be encrypted by conventional cryptographic means. This would improve the level of system security, since an attacker must gain the access to the encryption keys first. However, most privacy issues associated with a large database remain, since the keys and, therefore, the biometric data, are controlled by a custodian.[x]

A comprehensive review of the issues involving biometrics and cryptography can be found elsewhere.[xi]

4   What is Biometric Encryption (BE)?

Because of its variability, the biometric image or template itself cannot serve as a cryptographic key. However, the amount of information contained in a biometric image is quite large: for example, a typical image of 300x400 pixel size, encoded with eight bits per pixel has 300x400x8 = 960,000 bits of information. Of course, this information is highly redundant. One can ask a question: Is it possible to consistently extract a relatively small number of bits, say 128, out of these 960,000 bits without storage of any additional data? Or, is it possible to bind a 128-bit key to the biometric information, so that the key could be consistently regenerated? While the answer to the first question is problematic, the second question has given rise to the new area of research, called Biometric Encryption (BE).[1]

Biometric Encryption is a process that securely binds a PIN or a cryptographic key to a biometric, so that neither the key nor the biometric can be retrieved from the

---

[1] Other terms used for these technologies: biometric cryptosystem, private template, fuzzy commitment scheme, fuzzy vault, fuzzy extractor, secure sketch, biometric locking, biometric key binding, biometric key generation, virtual PIN, biometrically hardened passwords, biometric signature, etc. We use the term "Biometric Encryption" in a broad sense to include all the foregoing technologies.

stored template. The key is re-created only if the correct live biometric sample is presented on verification.

The digital key (password, PIN, etc.) is randomly generated on enrolment, so that nobody, including the user, knows it. The key itself is completely independent of biometrics and, therefore, can always be changed or updated. After a biometric sample is acquired, the BE algorithm securely and consistently binds the key to the biometric to create a protected BE template, also called a "private template." In essence, the key is encrypted with the biometric. The BE template provides an excellent privacy protection and can be stored either in a database or locally (on a smart card, token, laptop, cell phone, or other device.). At the end of the enrolment, both the key and the biometric are discarded.

On verification, the user presents her fresh biometric sample, which, when applied to the legitimate BE template, will let the BE algorithm retrieve the same key/password. So the biometric serves as a decryption key. At the end of verification, the biometric sample is discarded once again.

The BE algorithm is designed to account for acceptable variations in the input biometric. Nevertheless, an attacker whose biometric sample is different enough will not be able to retrieve the password. This encryption/decryption scheme is fuzzy, as the biometric sample is different each time, unlike an encryption key in conventional cryptography. Of course, it is a big technological challenge to make the system work.

After the digital key, password, PIN, etc., is retrieved, it can be used as the basis for any physical or logical application. The most obvious way lies in the conventional cryptosystem, such as a PKI, where the password will generate a pair of public and private keys.

Overall, Biometric Encryption is an effective, secure, and privacy friendly tool for biometric password management, since the biometric and the password are bound on a fundamental level.

5   Advantages of Biometric Encryption

Biometric Encryption technologies have enormous potential to enhance privacy and security. Some of the key benefits and advantages of this technology include:

5.1   NO retention of the biometric image or template

Most privacy and security concerns derive from storage and misuse of the biometric data.

A common concern is that "if you build it (the database), they will come (for the data)." The top-line privacy and security concerns include fears of potential data matching, surveillance, profiling, interception, data security breaches, and identity theft by others. Misuse and mismanagement of biometric data by others invokes negative externalities and costs that fall primarily upon individuals rather than the collecting organization. But the accountability and credibility of the collecting organization are also at stake and, with them, the viability of the entire program.

From a privacy perspective, the best practice is to collect little or no personally identifiable information (PII) at all in the first place. This is referred to as "data minimization" — minimizing the amount of personal data collected and retained, thus eliminating the possibility of subsequent abuse.

Biometric Encryption directly addresses these risks, threats and concerns. Users retain complete (local) control and use of their own biometrics. Local control enhances confidence and trust in the system, which ultimately promotes greater enrolment and use.

5.2   2. Multiple/cancelable/revocable identifiers

Biometric Encryption allows individuals to use a single biometric for multiple accounts and purposes without fear that these separate identifiers or uses will be linked together by a single biometric image or template. If a single account identifier becomes compromised, there is far less risk that all the other accounts will also be compromised. Even better, Biometric Encryption technologies make it possible to change or recompute account identifiers. That is, identifiers may be revoked or cancelled, and substituted for newly generated ones calculated from the same biometric! Traditional biometric systems simply cannot do this.

5.3   3. Improved authentication security: stronger binding of user biometric and identifier

Account identifiers are bound with the biometric and recomputed directly from it on verification. This results in much stronger account identifiers (passwords) that are longer and more complex, don't need to be memorized, and are less susceptible to security attacks. Many security vulnerabilities of a biometric system listed in Fig. 1 are also addressed by BE:

No substitution attack: An attacker cannot create his own template since neither he, nor anybody else, know the digital key and other transitory data used to create the legitimate template.

No tampering: Since the extracted features are not stored, the attacker has no way to modify them.

No high level masquerade attack: Again, the system does not store the biometric template, so that the attacker cannot create a digital artefact to submit to the system[2]. BE provides an effective protection for remote authentication systems.

---

[2] A masquerade attack may still be possible on a low level, which requires thorough knowledge of BE algorithm from an attacker. See, for example, "Hill Climbing" attack against an early BE system with insufficient protection[xxi].

No Trojan horse attacks: A BE algorithm does not use any score, either final or intermediate, to make a decision, it just retrieves (or does not retrieve) a key. Therefore, the attacker cannot fool the system by outputting a high score.

No overriding Yes/No response: The output of BE algorithm is a 128-bit (or longer) digital key, as opposed to the binary Yes/No response. The attacker cannot obtain the key from a private template.

The security of Biometric Encryption technology can be augmented by the use of tokens (e.g. smart cards, PDA) and additional passwords, if needed[xii].

5.4 Improved security of personal data and communications

As an added bonus, users can take advantage of the convenience and ease of BE technologies to encrypt their own personal or sensitive data. See Use Case Scenario #1 for an example. Since the key is one's own biometric, used locally, this technology could place a powerful tool directly in the hands of individuals. Biometric Encryption could be viewed as encryption for the masses, made easy!

5.5 Greater public confidence, acceptance, and use; greater compliance with privacy laws

Public confidence and trust are necessary ingredients for the success of any biometric system deployment. One major data breach involving a large centralized database of biometric templates could set back the entire industry for years.

Data governance policies and procedures can only go so far to foster public trust. However, if privacy, security and trust can be built directly into the biometric system, then the public and data protection authorities are far more likely to accept the privacy claims being made.

Putting biometric data firmly under the exclusive control of the individual, in a way that benefits that individual and minimizes risk of surveillance and identity theft, will go a long way towards satisfying the requirements of privacy and data protection laws, and will promote broader acceptance and use of biometrics.

5.6 Suitable for large-scale applications

BE technologies speak directly to the clear preference and recommendations of international privacy and data protection authorities for using biometrics to authenticate or verify identity, rather than for identification purposes alone.

We prefer to see biometrics used to positively link the bearer to a card or token, avoiding the creation of systems that rely upon centralized storage and remote access/lookup of biometric data. An important reason for this view is that it is not known if biometric technology is sufficiently accurate and reliable to permit real time identification in large n samples, where n is of an order of several million or higher. Nevertheless, many large-scale one-to-many public biometric projects are being proposed and are well underway.

Often the biometric data in these systems are actually used for authentication purposes and not identification, but the lines between these two concepts can be blurred when multiple data items are collected and transmitted to a database for comparison. The distinction between the identifier and the authenticator can be somewhat arbitrary.

From a privacy point of view, transmitting biometric image or template data to a central database to be authenticated is risky enough without compounding the risks by sending more and more personal identifiers with it. Multimodal biometric solutions depend on collecting and comparing more than one biometric. It should be noted that the main reason for using multimodal solutions, besides providing a fallback for problem users, is insufficient accuracy/speed/security of existing biometrics. So the technical solution to using biometrics for authentication seems to be to collect more and more biometric and other personal data.

The European Data Protection Supervisor (EDPS) Peter Hustinx has warned, in his commentaries and formal opinions, of the privacy dangers of using biometric images or templates as an index or key to interoperable databases.[xiii]

Fortunately, BE technologies make possible database applications, minimizing the risks of traditional biometric systems (although we still prefer one-to-one applications with local template storage). It is possible to create secure and local biometric-enabled bindings of users to some other token identifiers without the need to reveal the actual biometric image or data.

It is further possible to create a so-called "anonymous database" where a link between an anonymous identifier and encrypted (by conventional cryptographic means) user's record is controlled by a BE process. This is very useful for a database containing sensitive information, such as medical records (see Use Case Scenario #2).

Another promising application of BE is a privacy-protected one-to-many database for preventing "double dipping." The database is multimodal: it contains conventional but anonymous templates for one biometric (e.g. fingerprints) and private templates (e.g. for iris) that control the link with the user's encrypted records. A user's record would only be decrypted and displayed if there was a positive match on both conventional and private templates. Otherwise, all the information is inaccessible even to the system administrator.

With Biometric Encryption, users would be empowered by the ability to securely prove who they are to anyone, for any purpose, using their own biometrics, without having to disclose the biometric data itself.

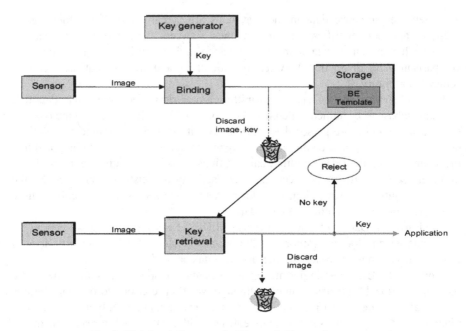

Fig. 2. High level diagram of a Biometric Encryption process

The enrolment part of a BE system consists of at least four blocks: a biometric sensor, a key generator that normally outputs a random key, a binding algorithm that creates a BE (private) template, and a storage for the BE template. Neither the key nor the image can be recovered from the BE template. The key, the image, and some transitory data are discarded at the end of the enrolment process.

The verification part contains at least a sensor to acquire a new image sample, and a key retrieval algorithm, which applies the image to the previously enrolled BE template received from the storage. The algorithm either retrieves the key, if the image on verification is close enough to the one enrolled, or fails to do so, in which case the user is rejected. The key enters an application, such as a PKI. Each application has its unique key. The biometric image is discarded at the end of the verification process.

6   Current State of Biometric Encryption

The original concept of Biometric Encryption for fingerprints was pioneered in 1994 by Dr. George Tomko, founder of Mytec Technologies (Toronto, Canada). Since then, many research groups have taken part in the development of BE and related technologies. There is substantial number of articles and patents published to date, most of which have appeared since 2002.[i]

BE and related technologies have drawn attention from major academic research groups specializing in biometrics and industry leaders..

Virtually all types of biometrics have been tested to bind (or generate) a digital key: fingerprints, iris, face, keystroke dynamics, voice, handwritten signatures, and palm prints. The most promising results have been achieved with iris, where FRR = 0.47%, FAR = 0 (or at least less than one in 200,000) to generate a 140-bit key[xiv]. These error rates are only marginally higher than for a conventional iris-based biometric system with the same input images.[3]

The use of fingerprints is also feasible in terms of accuracy for BE, with FRR greater than 10% at present[xii]. Unlike an iris, there is a noticeable degradation in accuracy from a conventional fingerprint system. This is understandable since fingerprints are more prone to distortions and other factors that degrade accuracy. It is more difficult to compensate those factors in the case of Biometric Encryption, since BE works in a "blind" mode (the enrolled fingerprint or its minutiae template are not seen). There are several ways to overcome this problem, for example, by using a free air (i.e., contactless) fingerprint sensor, or by using more than one finger from the same person, or by combining several biometrics. Note that even a 10% – 20% false rejection rate may still be acceptable for some applications with relatively low traffic and cooperative users: it simply means that a person would be rejected each fifth or tenth time on average and asked by the system to place the finger on the reader again.

Face recognition, which is usually considered third (after irises and fingerprints) in terms of accuracy in conventional biometrics, has shown a significant improvement of performance over the last few years. This allowed Philips Research to create a working BE system using a face biometric. The published results range from FRR = 3.5% for a face database with low to medium variability of images to FRR = 35% for a database with high variability; FAR = 0 (or at least less than 1 in 100,000) in both cases. The key size used is 58 bits, which may be sufficient as a password replacement. The Philips technology, called privID[TM], is a part of a European 3D Face project [xv].

It is not clear if other biometrics have enough entropy (i.e., the amount of non-redundant information) to bind a sufficiently long key (e.g. 128 bit). This is an area of future research.

Some works published since 2002 provide a general theoretical foundation for BE technologies from a cryptographic point of view. They prove that the system can be made secure against "brute force" search attacks. In other words, an attacker checks at random all possible combinations in order to retrieve a key (or a biometric). Like conventional cryptography, it is assumed that the attacker is fully familiar with the algorithm, and may have a template in hand, but does not have a proper biometric to unlock the secret (i.e., the key bound to the biometric).

However, the attacker may try more sophisticated attacks exploiting inherent weaknesses (if any) of the BE system and biometrics in general. This area of research has been largely overlooked. If such an attack were successful, the effective security of the system would be reduced from 128 bits to, perhaps, 69, 44, or an even lower number of bits. "This may seem an alarmingly small number to the crypto purist."[xiv]

---

[3] The iris images were acquired in close to ideal conditions of a laboratory environment. In real life systems, some degradation of performance is expected, which is always the case with biometrics.

On the other hand, BE is not just another cryptographic algorithm; it is rather a key/password management scheme. Key management has always been the weakest part of any cryptosystem, as it relies on passwords that may be forgotten, stolen, guessed, shared, etc. Biometric Encryption binds the key/password with the biometric and, thus, makes the system more secure.

It is interesting to note that breaking a biometrically encrypted key exposes that key, but not necessarily the biometric, let alone the entire BE database, making it a more secure system.

With the notable exception of Philips privID^{TM}, to the best of our knowledge, there is no commercially available BE system being used to date. The reason for this lies in both the technological challenges and market conditions. Not only the general public, but most hi-tech developers, are unaware of this emerging technology. Consequently, resources and funding in this area have, to date, been poor. We believe that the technological challenges have been overcome to a large extent using an iris, and partially for face and fingerprints, so that the BE technology is very close to the prototype development stage and could soon be ready for testing in pilot projects.

7   Related Technologies

7.1   Storing a key in a trusted system

There have been some products that store a cryptographic key or a PIN in a so-called trusted system (e.g. a computer or a Digital Signal Processor (DSP)). The key is released upon successful biometric verification and then enters a conventional cryptosystem, e.g. Public Key Infrastructure (PKI). The biometric template (or image) is also stored somewhere, often in encrypted (by conventional means) form.

If properly implemented, such systems may offer some security benefits. However, most problems outlined in the foregoing sections remain. For example, a binary Yes/No response is still required to release the key – this part of the algorithm is just hidden better. Most privacy issues associated with the template storage are also there.

Note that these systems often use the same terminology and/or claim the same benefits as BE, while in fact they do not provide a true binding between a key and a biometric.

7.2   Cancelable biometrics

A new area of research, closely related to BE, is cancelable biometrics. It has been developed by IBM T.J. Watson Research Center, and by some academic groups[xvi]. In this privacy-protecting technology, a distortion transform (preferably, irreversible) is applied to a biometric template. Only those distorted templates are stored, and they are matched also in the distorted form. If a distorted template is compromised, it can be "cancelled" by choosing just another distortion transform (i.e., the biometric is not lost). The transforms are application-dependent, meaning that the templates cannot be reused by another applications (so function creep is prevented).

Cancelable biometrics has some other similarities with BE, for example, a technique called bioHashing can be used for both technologies. But unlike BE, a key is not generated or released in cancelable biometrics, so that the system still produces a binary Yes/No response and is more vulnerable to attacks. The distortion transform should be truly irreversible (i.e., one way only) and kept secret. Otherwise, an attacker can either reconstruct the original biometric or create his own impostor template for a substitution attack, or even create an "artefact" image for a masquerade attack. Since the key is not generated, the variety of potential applications is narrower than for BE; for example, an anonymous database cannot be created. On the other hand, BE possesses all the functionality of cancelable biometrics. Both technologies face similar accuracy/security challenges.

7.3   Fuzzy Identity Based Encryption

Another related technology, called Fuzzy Identity Based Encryption (FIBE), was proposed by A. Sahai and B. Waters in 2005[xvii]. This technology also combines biometrics and cryptography on a fundamental level. Unlike BE, the user's biometric is made somewhat public. In an example provided by D. Nali, C. Adams and A. Miri[xviii], a user (A) could go to a Driver Licensing Agency (D), and identify herself via an iris scan, under the ongoing surveillance of a trained agent. D could then use this scan to encrypt A's information (e.g. an annual driver's license), when this information needs to be securely sent to A (e.g. via the Web). In order to obtain her biometric private keys, A would have to go in-person to a trusted third party (e.g. a state agency) that would deliver keys via the same authenticating procedure as that used by D. A could then decrypt the message addressed to her using FIBE. She does not need a biometric reading at that point. In other words, A leaves her biometrics in at least two places, D and the trusted third party (often called Trusted Authority (TA)).

This scheme prevents impersonation of A by surreptitious capturing of her biometric sample, such as an iris photograph or latent fingerprints. "FIBE allows biometric measurements to be public"[xviii] and, therefore, those surreptitious samples would become useless. While interesting from a scientific point of view, this technology is not privacy protecting, as biometric data are considered personal information. There are also problems in handling a false rejection: user A may not have a chance to present another biometric sample if the false rejection occurs during decryption.

8   Scientific, Technological, and Privacy-Related Merits

Encryption with a fuzzy key (such as a biometric) was only recently introduced in conventional cryptography. Beyond such trivial things like accepting a few spelling errors in a password, or letting Alice partially share a list of her favourite movies with Bob, Biometric Encryption technologies are by far the most important application of those theoretical works. Market demand for such a technology would provide a great incentive to this promising area of modern mathematics and cryptography.

BE results in tougher requirements for distortion tolerance, discrimination, and the security of a biometric system. Solving these problems would be a significant scientific breakthrough both in the area of biometrics and cryptography. This would accelerate research and development of better biometric sensors and other hardware, as well as new, more accurate algorithms and software. No doubt this would bring technological benefits for the entire field of biometrics.

BE overcomes many security vulnerabilities of a biometric system, especially in a distributed environment. This could facilitate deployment of biometric systems on portable and handheld devices (laptops, cellphones, PDAs, etc.).

It would not be an overstatement to say that biometrics is perceived, in general, as a privacy-invasive technology. As we have shown, this perception is not baseless. Biometric Encryption, on the other hand, is a privacy-enhancing technology. It allows a user to retain full control over her biometric and, at the same time, to stay anonymous in many applications, i.e., to be represented only by a randomly generated (and cancelable) identifier linked to her biometric. No other personal data, e.g. address, telephone, date of birth, have to be revealed.

BE can render databases privacy-protected, as they will comprise "private templates." While such databases cannot be used for a background check, they are perfectly suitable for one-to-one access control systems or even for systems that prevent multiple registrations and related fraud. The user retains control over his or her sensitive information, such as medical or financial records, stored in the database.

Proliferation of BE technology may ultimately change the public's perception of biometrics. This would raise the benchmark for biometric technologies, such that the industry would be prompted to develop and adopt new privacy-friendly solutions. If the "private templates" generated by BE make a significant presence in the market, this could reshape the entire biometric industry. Increased user acceptance and confidence would be extremely beneficial for the industry.

8.1   Use Case Scenario #1: Small-scale use of BE

To demonstrate the power of BE, we will briefly present a biometric authentication protocol (remote or local) with third party certification. We use a simplified and reworded description from Boyen's paper on fuzzy extractors.[xix]

Suppose that Alice wishes to authenticate herself to Bob using biometrics. Due to privacy concerns, she does not wish to reveal any biometric information to Bob. Conversely, for the authentication to be meaningful, Bob wants some assurance that Alice is, in fact, in possession of her purported biometrics at the time the authentication is taking place (i.e., that no one is impersonating her). We assume that there is a third party (often called the Trusted Authority), Trent, whom Bob trusts to honestly certify Alice's biometrics, and to whom Alice will temporarily grant access to her biometrics for the purpose of generating such a certificate. Alice will want to be able to obtain as many or as few of those certificates as she wants, and to reuse as many of them with multiple Bobs, some of whom may even be dishonest, without fear of privacy leaks or impersonation. The protocol is as follows:

Enrolment and certification takes place under Trent's supervision and using Alice's own biometric, as follows:

1. Alice creates a BE template from her biometric and a randomly selected PIN. Neither the biometric nor the PIN can be recovered from the template.
2. The PIN is used to generate a pair of keys called public and private keys.
3. The biometric, the PIN, and the private key are discarded.
4. If Trent is satisfied that Alice has executed the steps honestly, he certifies the binding between Alice's name and the public key, i.e., he digitally signs the pair ["Alice," public key]. At this point, Alice may send the public key to Bob, or even publish it for all to see.

A challenge/response scheme is used to verify Alice:

1. At any time when appropriate (e.g. whenever Alice desires to authenticate herself to Bob), Bob sends Alice a fresh random challenge.
2. By obtaining her new biometric sample and applying it to her BE template, Alice recovers her PIN on the fly, which, in turn, regenerates her private key.
3. Alice signs the challenge with her private key and gives Bob the signature.
4. Bob authenticates Alice by checking the validity of the signature under her authentic public key.

The protocol does not require Alice to remember or store her PIN or her private key. The BE template may be stored on a smart card or in Alice's laptop that also has a biometric sensor. For different applications ("multiple Bobs"), a new pair of public and private keys is generated from the PIN. Those keys are periodically updated. Some applications may require different PINs, in which case several BE templates can be stored. A proper template can be automatically recognized by the application.

The system based on digital signatures may be adopted both for a remote and local access. The important point is that the most critical part of any cryptosystem, the PIN (or a password), is securely bound to the biometrics.

To summarize, Alice has in her possession and under her control as many BE templates as necessary. She can use them to digitally sign in, either for remote authentication or for logical or physical access. The authentication is done simply by checking the validity of her digital signature using standard cryptographic means. Neither Alice's biometric nor her PIN are stored or revealed. As a result, the system is both secure and highly privacy-protective.

8.2   Use Case Scenario #2:

Anonymous database; large or medium-scale applications

Suppose that a clinic, a hospital, or a network of hospitals maintains a database of medical records. Alice does not want her record to be accessed by unauthorized personnel or third parties, even for statistical purposes. For that the latter, her record is made anonymous and encrypted (by conventional means). The only public entry in the database is her personal identifier, which may be her real name or, in certain cases (e.g. drug addiction clinic), an alias ("Jane Doe"). The link between Alice's identifier and her medical record is controlled by Biometric Encryption.

On enrolment, a BE template is created from Alice's biometric and a randomly-generated PIN (Alice does not even know the PIN). The PIN is used to generate a pointer to Alice's medical record and a crypto-key that encrypts the record, and also a pair of keys called public and private keys (similar to Use Case Scenario #1). The BE template and the public key are associated with Alice's ID and stored in the database (they can be also stored on Alice's smart card). Other temporary data, such as Alice's biometric, the PIN, the private key, the pointer, and the crypto-key, are discarded.

Suppose that Alice visits a doctor, to whom she wants to grant remote access to her medical record, or part of it, if the record is structured. From the doctor's office, Alice makes a request to the database administrator, Bob. The authentication procedure using challenge/response scheme is similar to that in use case scenario #1:

1. If Alice does not have her smart card with her (e.g. in the case of an emergency), Bob sends Alice's BE template to the doctor's office.
2. Alice applies her new biometric sample to the BE template and recovers her PIN on the fly.
3. The PIN is used to regenerate her private key, the pointer to her medical record, and the crypto-key.
4. Bob sends Alice a fresh random challenge.
5. Alice signs the challenge with her private key and gives Bob the signature.
6. Bob authenticates Alice by checking the validity of the signature under her public key.
7. Alice securely sends Bob the pointer to her medical record.
8. Bob recovers Alice's encrypted medical record (or a part of it, also encrypted) and sends it to Alice.
9. Using her crypto-key, which was regenerated from her PIN, Alice decrypts her medical record for the doctor.
10. Alice's biometric, the PIN, the private key, the pointer, and the crypto-key, are discarded.

In summary, Bob (the database administrator) has an assurance that Alice is, in fact, who she claims to be (she was able to unlock her BE template in the doctor's office); he is also assured that her medical record was sent to the right person. At the same time, Alice retains full control over her medical record, so that even Bob (the database administrator) has no access to it, since he does not have the crypto-key to decrypt it. The privacy protection is embedded into the system at a very basic technological level.

8.3   Use Case Scenario #3:

Travel documents; large-scale database applications

Using biometrics for travel documents has been a hot topic of discussion of late. To illustrate how BE can protect the user's privacy and, at the same time, improve the level of security, we will consider a system proposed by Van der Veen et al.[xx]

The International Civil Aviation Organization (ICAO) dictates international standards for Machine Readable Travel Documents (MRTD), including those for ePassports. Among the recommendations is the "three-way-check" for secure verification at a border crossing. This involves comparing data originating from (i) the biometric sensor, (ii) the biometric image stored on the ePassport, and (iii) biometric data stored in external (centralized) databases.

BE technology provides the opportunity to do this in a privacy preserving manner. In addition to the biometric templates stored on the ePassport, their secure versions, namely, the BE templates, are also stored in a third-party database. The biometric images or conventional templates are not stored in the database. A "three-way check" is then performed by matching the BE template from the database to that appearing on the ePassport, and the live biometric measurement scanned at the kiosk. So border passage now involves the following steps:

1.   At a kiosk, a user claims his identity (ID), and presents his biometric (e.g. facial image, fingerprint or iris) for measurements.
2.   The ID is sent to the third-party database to extract the corresponding BE template.
3.   The BE template is transmitted to the kiosk.
4.   The BE template and the biometric measurement are combined to derive a hashed version of the cryptographic key.
5.   The image of the iris, face or fingerprint is extracted from the ePassport and used together with the BE template to derive another hashed version of the cryptographic key. This will validate the biometric stored on the ePassport.
6.   Both hashed versions of the key derived in Steps 4 and 5 are transmitted to the border control authority and verified against the database version. A positive authentication is achieved when all three versions are identical.

The user's privacy is protected since the biometric image or template is not stored in a central database; instead, a secure BE template is stored. The database is inherently secure, meaning there is no need for complicated encryption and key management protocols. The ePassport is protected against tampering, since neither a potential attacker nor anybody else know the cryptographic key that was used to create the BE template.

9   Next Steps for Bringing BE to the Prototype Stage

Biometric Encryption has been researched since the mid-90s. Technologically, this area is much more challenging than conventional biometrics. But now, BE is fast approaching the next phase, i.e., the creation and testing of a prototype. The following issues still need to be addressed:

9.1   Selecting a Proper Biometric

The most promising results in terms of accuracy have been obtained for irises. Low variability of image samples, and the presence of a natural alignment feature (the pupil), make this biometric the number one candidate for BE.

Face recognition is the most publicly acceptable type of biometric. Recent advances in the technology made it possible to use face biometric for BE. At the present time, one of the drawbacks of the face-based BE system, however, is the relatively small size (~ 58 bits) of the encryption key that may be securely bound to the biometric. Using high resolution or 3D face recognition would likely improve the system performance.

Fingerprints, for which the BE was originally pioneered, are also a prime choice. The fingerprint biometric is used more widely than the iris, and most privacy concerns relate to fingerprints. At the same time, using fingerprints for BE turns out to be much more challenging. The reasons are that high skin distortions can be introduced when the finger presses upon the sensor, and the difficulty of aligning a fingerprint on verification with the one enrolled. As mentioned before, the situation is more difficult for BE than for a conventional fingerprint verification, since most BE schemes work in a "blind" mode (the enrolled fingerprint or its minutiae template are not seen). Some of these issues can be overcome with a free-air image. Although this would present other optical issues, we believe they could be resolved by current technology. In general, face and especially iris are less vulnerable to distortion and alignment problems.

Other biometrics, e.g. voice, signature, palmprints, etc., may not have enough entropy (i.e., the amount of non-redundant information to support a long enough cryptographic key). They could be possibly put on the list of "auxiliary" biometrics, i.e., used for BE in combination with irises, faces, or fingerprints or, perhaps, with conventional passwords (which is called "hardening").

9.2   Improving the Image Acquisition Process

For fingerprints, this means choosing a proper fingerprint sensor that is less susceptible to skin distortions (e.g. a free air sensor), or changing the existing sensor ergonomics to keep the distortions under control. Image quality can also be improved at the algorithm level (i.e., through software). In general, the requirements for the image quality are tougher for BE than for conventional biometrics.

9.3   Making BE Resilient Against Attacks

This area of research — the analysis of potential vulnerability of BE against attacks— has been largely overlooked. By that we mean that a sophisticated attacker could gain access to both the BE templates and the algorithm. The only thing he cannot obtain is a user's biometric. Such an attacker, fully familiar with the algorithm and exploiting its weaknesses, will not be doing just a brute force search (i.e., about 2128 computations for a 128 bit key) in order to break the BE template. Instead, he will devise various attacks that can be run in a realistic time frame. The BE algorithm must be resilient against those off-line attacks[xxi]. The same approach (i.e., resilience against attacks) is adopted in conventional cryptography.

9.4   Improving Accuracy and Security of BE Algorithm

There have been substantial advances in algorithm development in conventional biometrics in the past few years, as demonstrated by a series of international competitions. Many of those advances are applicable to BE.

For BE, a crucial step, both in terms of accuracy and security, is selection of a proper *Error Correcting Code* (ECC). For the past 10-13 years, there have been major advances in the area of ECC. Some of them have been already applied to BE with promising results[xxii].

9.5   Exploiting Multimodal Approaches

This has been a hot area of research and development in conventional biometrics. The performance of a biometric system is significantly improved when different algorithms, or different fingers, or different biometrics (e.g. fingerprints and face) are combined. The modes that are combined should be "orthogonal" i.e., statistically independent. It is reasonable to expect that the multimodal approach would also work for BE.

9.6   Developing BE Applications

The applications, such as those described in the case studies, should clearly demonstrate the benefits for privacy and security brought about by the use of BE.

10 Summary and Conclusions

Biometric Encryption technology is a fruitful area for research and has become sufficiently mature for broader public policy consideration, prototype development, and consideration of applications.

This paper has explored the possibilities and privacy-enhancing benefits of Biometric Encryption technologies for meeting the needs of businesses and government agencies.

We believe that BE technology exemplifies the fundamental privacy and data protection principles endorsed around the world, such as data minimization, user empowerment and security, better than any other biometric technology solution in existence.

We hope that our paper will form a valuable contribution to current national and international discussions regarding the most appropriate methods to achieve, in a privacy-enhanced manner, strong identification and authentication protocols.

While introducing biometrics into information systems may result in considerable benefits, it can also introduce many new security and privacy vulnerabilities, risks, and concerns, as discussed above. However, novel Biometric Encryption techniques have been developed that can overcome many, if not most, of those risks and vulnerabilities, resulting in a win-win, positive-sum scenario.

One can only hope that the biometric portion is done well, and preferably not modeled on a zero-sum paradigm, where there must always be a loser. A positive-sum model, in the form of Biometric Encryption, presents distinct advantages to both security and privacy.

References

[i] See list of resources in appendices of: Ann Cavoukian and Alex Stoianov, *Biometric Encryption: A Positive-Sum Technology that Achieves Strong Authentication, Security AND Privacy* (March 2007) at www.ipc.on.ca/images/Resources/up-1bio_encryp.pdf, and: Organization for Economic Co-operation and Development (OECD), Directorate for Science, Technology and Industry (DSTI), Committee for Information, Computer and Communications Policy (ICCP): *Biometric-Based Technologies* DSTI/ICCP/REG(2003)2/FINAL (June 2004); and

International Biometric Group BioPrivacy Initiative at www.Bioprivacy.org

[ii] See the 27th International Conference of Data Protection and Privacy Commissioners, Montreux, Switzerland, *Resolution on the use of biometrics in passports, identity cards and travel documents* (16 Sept 2005).

[iii] See European Union Article 29 Working Party, *Working document on biometrics* (Aug 2003)

[iv] See: UK Information Commissioner, *Data Protection Technical Guidance Note: Privacy enhancing technologies* (Nov 2006);

European Commission, Communication: Promoting Data Protection by Privacy Enhancing Technologies (PETs) (COM(2007) 228 final) (May 02, 2007); and

Information and Privacy Commissioner of Ontario & Dutch Registratiekamer, *Privacy-Enhancing Technologies: The Path to Anonymity* (Vols I & II - August 1995)

[v] For excellent overviews and discussions of PETs, see:

OECD DSTI/ICCP, *Inventory of Privacy-Enhancing Technologies (PETs)* (Jan 2003)

Dutch Interior Ministry, *Privacy-Enhancing Technologies. White paper for decision-makers* (2004)

R. Leenes, J. Schallaböck and M. Hansen, Privacy and Identity Management for Europe (PRIME) Project, *PRIME White paper v2* (June 2007)

Future of Identity in the Information Society (FIDIS) Project, *D13.1: Identity and impact of privacy enhancing technologies* (2007)

[vi] N. K. Ratha, J. H. Connell, R. M. Bolle. Enhancing security and privacy in biometrics-based authentication systems. IBM Systems Journal, vol. 40, NO 3, p.p. 614 – 634, 2001

[vii] C.J. Hill, "Risk of masquerade arising from the storage of biometrics," B.S. Thesis, Australian National University, 2001 (supervisor Dr. Roger Clarke).

[viii] R. Cappelli, A. Lumini, D. Maio, and D. Maltoni, "Fingerprint Image Reconstruction from Standard Templates". IEEE Transactions On Pattern Analysis And Machine Intelligence, v. 29, No. 9, pp. 1489 - 1503, 2007

[ix] B. Schneier, "The Uses and Abuses of Biometrics," Comm. ACM, vol. 42, no. 8, p. 136, Aug. 1999

[x] There has been recent activity of International Organization for Standardization in order to support the confidentiality and integrity of the biometric template by using cryptographic means (ISO/IEC WD 24745, "Biometric Template Protection").

[xi] FIDIS report, "D3.2: A study on PKI and biometrics," 2005

[xii] K. Nandakumar, A. Nagar, and A. K. Jain, "Hardening Fingerprint Fuzzy Vault Using Password", Proceedings of ICB 2007, Seoul, Korea, August 27-29, 2007. Lecture Notes in Computer Science, Springer, v. 4642, pp. 927-937, 2007

[xiii] See EDPS, Comments on the Communication of the Commission on interoperability of European Databases (10 March 2006)

[xiv] F. Hao, R. Anderson, and J. Daugman. "Combining Crypto with Biometrics Effectively". IEEE Transactions on Computers, v. 55, No.9, pp. 1081-1088, 2006

[xv] www.3Dface.org

[xvi] N. K. Ratha, S. Chikkerur, J. H. Connell, and R. M. Bolle, "Generating Cancelable Fingerprint Templates". IEEE Transactions On Pattern Analysis And Machine Intelligence, v. 29, No. 4, pp. 561-572, 2007; and the references cited there.

[xvii] A. Sahai and B. Waters, "Fuzzy identity based encryption," in Proceedings of EUROCRYPT'05 on Advances in Cryptology, LNCS 3494, pp. 457–473, Springer-Verlag, 2005

[xviii] D. Nali, C. Adams, and A. Miri. Using Threshold Attribute-Based Encryption for Practical Biometric-Based Access Control. International Journal of Network Security, Vol.1, No.3, pp.173–182, Nov. 2005

[xix] X. Boyen, "Reusable cryptographic fuzzy extractors," CCS 2004, pp. 82–91, ACM Press.

[xx] M. van der Veen, T. Kevenaar, G.-J. Schrijen, T. H. Akkermans, and Fei Zuo, "Face Biometrics with Renewable Templates". Proceedings of SPIE, Volume 6072: Security, Steganography, and Watermarking of Multimedia Contents VIII, 2006.

[xxi] A. Adler, "Vulnerabilities in biometric encryption systems". NATO RTA Workshop: Enhancing Information Systems Security - Biometrics (IST-044-RWS-007), 2004

[xxii] S. C. Draper, A. Khisti, E. Martinian, A. Vetro and J. S. Yedidia, "Using Distributed Source Coding to Secure Fingerprint Biometrics". *Proc. of IEEE International Conference on Acoustics, Speech and Signal Processing (ICASSP)*, v. 2, pp. 129-132, April 2007

Investigating and Comparing Multimodal Biometric Techniques

Christopher Andrade and Sebastian H. von Solms

Academy for Information Technology
University of Johannesburg
Johannesburg, South Africa

Abstract. Determining the identity of a person has become vital in today's world. Emphasis on security has become increasingly more common in the last few decades, not only in Information Technology, but across all industries. One of the main principles of security is that a system only be accessed by a legitimate user. According to the ISO 7498/2 document [1] (an international standard which defines an information security system architecture) there are 5 pillars of information security. These are Identification/Authentication, Confidentiality, Authorization, Integrity and Non Repudiation. The very first line of security in a system is identifying and authenticating a user. This ensures that the user is who he/she claims to be, and allows only authorized individuals to access your system. Technologies have been developed that can automatically recognize a person by his unique physical features. This technology, referred to as 'biometrics', allows us to quickly, securely and conveniently identify an individual. Biometrics solutions have already been deployed worldwide, and it is rapidly becoming an acceptable method of identification in the eye of the public. As useful and advanced as unimodal (single biometric sample) biometric technologies are, they have their limits. Some of them aren't completely accurate; others aren't as secure and can be easily bypassed. Recently it has been reported to the congress of the U.S.A [2] that about 2 percent of the population in their country do not have a clear enough fingerprint for biometric use, and therefore cannot use their fingerprints for enrollment or verification. This same report recommends using a biometric system with dual (multimodal) biometric inputs, especially for large scale systems, such as airports. In this technical paper we will investigate and compare multimodal biometric techniques, in order to determine how much of an advantage lies in using this technology, over its unimodal equivalent.

1 Introduction

The use of biometric technologies – the mathematical analysis of a unique characteristic such as fingerprints, iris and retina – has been adopted worldwide and on a large scale. It is used in many different sectors, including government, banking, airports and schools. However, successful use of biometric systems in these areas does not automatically imply an ideal security system.

Please use the following format when citing this chapter:

Andrade, C. and von Solms, S. H., 2008, in IFIP International Federation for Information Processing, Volume 261; *Policies and Research in Identity Management*; Eds. E. de Leeuw, Fischer-Hübner, S., Tseng, J., Borking, J.; (Boston: Springer), pp. 79–90.

Most biometric systems are unimodal (i.e. they use only 1 biometric sample to recognize a user). Even the best unimodal biometric systems (usually iris, fingerprint and retina scanners) are far from perfect. They have many inherent problems in their use. The major dilemma is that no single biometric technology is perfectly suited for all applications. Furthermore, these unimodal technologies suffer from noisy sensor data, lack of individuality, non-universality, spoof attacks and included error rates in their use [3].

It is logical then, to try and combine multiple biometric samples to 'get the best of both worlds' so to speak. Some of the problems inherent in unimodal biometric systems can therefore be overcome by using multiple sources of information. Such systems are known as multimodal biometric systems. Multimodal biometric systems use 2 or more biometric samples from the same person in order to identify him/her.

These systems are then expected to be more accurate and less problematic because they take more independent pieces of evidence into account, before making a decision.

The purpose of this technical report is to determine if multimodal biometrics provide any significant improvement in accuracy over its unimodal counterpart.

Secondly, we will provide an objective analysis of available multimodal biometric fusion and normalization methods, to highlight their strengths and weaknesses, and to further explore their performance, relative to each other.

2   Multimodal Biometrics

Multimodal biometrics are systems that merge inputs obtained from two or more biometric sources. By combining these inputs from different sources, one can drastically improve the overall accuracy of the biometric system [3].

Multimodal biometric systems provide greater population coverage, because it is able to identify a person by more than just one unique identifier. Because of its improved security, it also discourages intruders to attempt to bypass or spoof the system. Adding more biometric checks makes it much more difficult for someone to simultaneously spoof different biometric traits.

A multimodal biometric system based on 2 or more biometric inputs is expected to be more resilient to noise, address problems of non universality (uniqueness of a biometric trait), increase matching accuracy, and increase security by making it harder for people to get away with spoof attacks.

These different inputs can come from a variety of sources [4]:

2.1   Multimodal biometric sources

- Single Trait/Multiple Classifiers: a single trait is used, but different classifiers are input to the system.
- Single Trait/Multiple Instances: again, a single trait is used, but similar inputs that are slightly different to one another are used.

- Single Trait/Multiple Units: a single trait is used, but different examples of it are input.
- Multiple Biometric Traits: here 2 different biometric traits are combined to verify or identify a user.

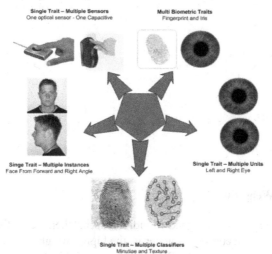

Fig. 1. Multimodal biometric sources.

3   Fusion

In order to join two biometric inputs, a method called 'fusion' is used. Fusion refers to the action of combining two separate biometric inputs (modalities).

Different fusion schemes exist. Following, is a list of the most common ones found and used in multimodal biometric systems today. [5] [6] [7]: Table 1 shows the representation of the variables:

Table 1. Symbol Representations for Fusion Schemes

Symbol	Representation
S_i	normalized input score
$i^{th}{}_i$	number of the matcher (1, 2, 3...)
N	total number of inputs
S_f	fused score

3.1   Simple-Sum:

$$S_f = \sum_{i=1}^{N} S_i$$

3.2   Min-Score:

$$S_f = \min(S_1, S_2 \ldots, S_N)$$

3.3   Max-Score:

$$S_f = \max(S_1, S_2 \ldots, S_N)$$

3.4   Matcher Weighting:

In this method, weights are assigned to individual matchers according to their Equal Error Rates. The more accurate a matcher is, the higher weight it is assigned, giving it more of a bias when it comes to the final fused score. Table 2 explains the variables:

Table 2. Symbol representations for fusion schemes.

Symbol	Representation
n_m^i	normalized input score
m	matcher
r^m	equal error rate
w^m	weight of input

$$w^m = \frac{(1/\sum_{m=1}^{M} \frac{1}{r^m})}{r^m}$$

Note:

$$0 \leq w^m \leq 1, \forall m, \sum_{m=1}^{M} w^m = 1$$

The formula then becomes:

$$S_f = \sum_{m=1}^{M} w^m n_i^m, \forall i$$

3.5   Sum of Probabilities:

We use $p(s \mid genuine)$ and $p(s \mid imposter)$ to evaluate:

$$P(genuine \mid S) = \frac{p(s \mid genuine)}{p(s \mid genuine) + p(s \mid imposter)}$$

In this method, the fused score is determined by the summation of the probability of true scores.

$$S_f = \sum_{i=1}^{N} P(genuine \mid S_i)$$

4   Normalization

Fusion works well if biometric scores are homogenous (i.e. of the same nature). However, if scores are non homogenous, then they require normalization to convert them into a range that makes them more similar to each other.

Normalization is usually necessary or preferred before the two biometric inputs are combined at the fusion point. Normalization simply refers to scores being converted into a more common domain. For example: If one matching module provides scores that are in the range of [10, 10 000] and another in the range of [0, 1], this becomes a problem.

Table 3. Symbol representation for normalization methods.

Symbol	Representation
s	Input Score
s'	Normalized Score
S	Total number of Inputs

4.1   Min-Max:

$$s' = \frac{s - \min(S)}{\max(S) - \min(S)}$$

4.2   Z-Score:

$$s' = \frac{s - mean(S)}{std(S)}$$

4.3   TanH:

$$s' = \frac{1}{2}[\tanh(0.01\frac{(s - mean(S))}{std(S)}) + 1]$$

4.4   Double Sigmoid Normalization:

$$s' = \frac{1}{1 + \exp(-2(\frac{s-t}{r1}))} \; if \cdot \cdot s < t$$

$$s' = \frac{1}{1 + \exp(-2(\frac{s-t}{r2}))} \; otherwise,$$

5   Practical Work

5.1   Scoresets

We have used the publicly available BSSR1 Scoreset, obtained from NIST (National Institute of Science and Technology) in the U.S.A. This is a set of generated similarity scores from two face recognition systems and one fingerprint system [8] In addition to using the BSSR1 scoreset, we have created our own database of biometric similarity scores. The score database consists of a small population (50 people) of face and finger scores.

5.2   FAR and FRR

In order for us to determine the accuracy of any biometric system, we have to measure the error rates. These are two key error rates in biometrics, false acceptance rate (FAR) and false rejection rate (FRR). We can measure these error rates by mapping a series of genuine scores and impostor scores onto a graph according to their frequency and score. In a perfect system, there will never be any overlap region of genuine scores and impostor scores – hence there will never be any "false accepts" or "false rejects". However, this never happens – no biometric system is 100% accurate.

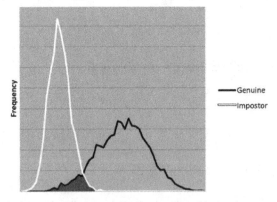

Fig. 2. An example of score distribution for a biometric system.

From Figure 2 we can see the two populations – one being genuine and one being impostor. The overlap region between these two populations is shaded in grey. It is apparent now that it is not easy to classify if a score is "genuine" or not when it falls into this overlap region. This is where the error rates - FRR and FAR tie into.

5.3   Genuine Acceptance Rate

Genuine Acceptance Rate (GAR) is an overall accuracy measurement of a biometric system. It is calculated by the formula: GAR = 1 – FRR [11]. GAR is important because it is the chief measurement of precision in this paper. Figure 3 below shows how GAR, FRR and FAR are linked:

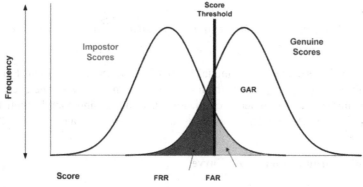

Fig. 3. FAR, FRR and GAR illustrated

FAR and GAR are usually mapped against each-other on a graph known as a ROC (Receiver Operating Characteristic) curve [12]. ROC curve's are used often in biometrics to compare the accuracy of a biometric matcher at a given confidence level (Example a FAR set to 1%).

5.4   Simple Sum Fusion - ROC Curve

Following is a ROC curve. It shows the performance of the simple sum fusion technique, paired with various normalization techniques.

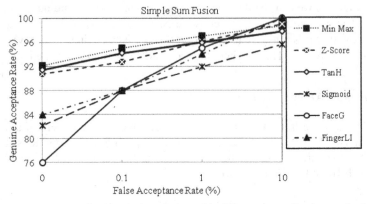

Fig. 4. ROC graph for Simple Sum fusion with different normalization methods.

We can clearly see that the unimodal biometric matchers (Face G and Finger LI) are outperformed by the majority of the multimodal techniques. With the exception of sigmoid normalization, the other normalization methods (using Simple Sum fusion) outperform the separate biometric systems – sometimes by up to a margin of 12%.

5.5   TanH Normalization ROC Curve

Following is a ROC curve (Figure 5), this time for the TanH normalization method, paired with the different fusion techniques.

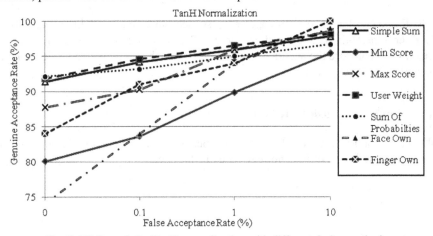

Fig. 5. ROC graph for TanH normalization with different fusion methods.

Again, it is clear from the graph that the unimodal biometrics are outperformed by their multimodal equivalents. In some areas, there exists almost a 15% gain in performance when using multimodal techniques.

5.6   Summary Performance Table

The table that follows is the combined average scores for all tested fusion and normalization methods. This table shows clear performance differences between these methods. The highlighted scores in bold show the highest performing fusion methods, paired with a normalization algorithm. The average performance of a fusion method is shown in the column on the right, while the average performance of a normalization method is shown in the column at the bottom.

Table 4 demonstrates all the methods at a False Acceptance Rate of 0, 1%:

Interpretation: at FAR of 0, 1% the Simple Sum fusion method is the most accurate, obtaining the highest GAR rate with 2 out of 4 normalization techniques. Simple Sum retains 1st place overall (Column on the right) for the best fusion method. TanH does the same (Column at the bottom) and is considered to be the most accurate. According to these results the Sigmoid normalization and Min Score fusion perform consistently in the lower range, and is considered the least accurate.

Table 4. GAR Performance at a FAR of 0. 1%.

Fusion Algorithms	Normalization Algorithms				
	Min Max	Z-Score	TanH	Sigmoid	Average Fusion
Simple Sum	**95.02**	**92.78**	94.20	87.93	**92.48**
Min Score	84.40	85.18	83.63	83.30	84.12
Max Score	84.48	88.26	90.28	**88.09**	87.7
Matcher Weight	95.00	89.74	**94.58**	87.99	91.82
Sum of Probabilities	94.17	86.97	93.17	85.26	89.89
Average Normalization	90.61	88.56	91.172	86.51	

5.7   Comments on Normalization Methods:

- *Min Max*: easy to use normalization method. Performs consistently well across all FAR ranges
- *Sigmoid*: complex normalization method. It produces very poor results – often worse than a single biometric.
- *Z-score*: quite a simple method to use. Consistently near the top performer in the practical experiments. It does not do well if input score is outside the range of original training scores.
- *TanH*: best overall normalization technique in practical tests. It adapts well to scores that fall outside the range of original training scores.

At a higher FAR (1%), Min-Max and TanH seem to perform the best. At a lower FAR of (0,1%) Z-Score catches up, and performs just as well and Min-Max and TanH.

If information such as minimum and maximum (for Min Max) and mean and standard deviation (for Z-Score) can be determined from the scores before hand, then these two normalization algorithms will work just fine. This is ideal in a closed environment such as a work place, where repeated biometric entries and their statistics can be collected. In open environments such as airports, TanH which is not sensitive to outlying data ranges, and adapts well, can be used as a normalization method.

5.8   Comments on Fusion Methods:

- *Min Score*: very simple to use, but performs consistently poorly.
- *Max Score*: also very simple to use – low to average performance.
- *Simple Sum*: easy to implement – practical tests show it to be the most accurate fusion method overall.
- *Matcher Weight*: strong performer. It relies on the weights being set very accurately according to the performance of the separate biometric readers. Sometimes the weights need to be 'played around' with to get the best performance out of this fusion method.
- *Sum of Probabilities*: very complex fusion method. It requires an accurate probability density function of genuine and impostor scores, and a thorough understanding of advanced statistics. If implemented correctly, it can produce good results.

At a higher FAR (1%) Simple Sum and Matcher Weight are at the top. At a lower FAR of (0.1%) Max Score and Sum of probabilities catch up and they all perform relatively evenly.

The easiest fusion method to use would be Simple Sum. It performs exceptionally well, and is simple to understand and use. Matcher weight is another fusion method that has very good accuracy, but again, it needs to be adjusted until a 'sweet spot' is found that delivers good performance.

The effort required to implement sum of probabilities doesn't make it worthwhile, especially considering that a trouble-free method such as simple sum performs even better.

6   Conclusion

The results clearly show that choosing the right fusion scheme and pairing it with the right normalization method, makes a significant impact on the resulting performance of a multimodal system.

The practical investigation also demonstrates the obvious improved accuracy of multimodal biometrics, over their unimodal counterparts.

The practical results have evidently revealed that Simple Sum and Matcher Weighting are the best performing fusion methods. TanH and Min-Max normalization methods were considered the most accurate.

We determined that Min-Max and Z-Score normalization would work best in closed-environments such as offices, and that a more flexible normalization scheme would be needed in open environments such as airports. Here TanH is best suited for the job.

We have learned that multimodal biometric systems may take a fair amount of time to setup initially, as training sets or data needed for the algorithms are gathered. This has proven to be a long process, especially in databases with large populations. However, once in place, multimodal biometric systems function just as speedily as their unimodal equivalent.

We have also shown in our own practical experimentation that by using a unimodal biometric source, many false users are let into a system (resulting from the unimodal error rates being higher than the multimodal ones). By using multimodal biometric systems, we can improve accuracy by cutting down on error rates. We also improve security as it is harder for an intruder to bypass multiple systems at once then it is to spoof a single one.

The biometric challenge has always been to create a system that is completely accurate and safe from intruders. Even the best unimodal biometric schemes by themselves have not accomplished this feat. With the introduction of multimodal biometrics as a technology, we are now moving towards that "perfect" recognition system, although we are not quite there yet.

While unimodal biometrics leaves an accuracy gap for multimodal biometric systems to fill, multimodal systems will always exist. The need then becomes to either further increase the accuracy of single biometric systems, or to ensure that multimodal systems become more mainstream.

References

1. ISO 7498-2 Information processing systems - Open Systems Interconnection Basic Reference Model -- Part 2: Security Architecture
2. NIST Report to the United States Congress - Summary of NIST Standards for Biometric Accuracy, Tamper Resistance, and Interoperability, November 13 2002.
3. Multibiometric Systems 34 January 2004/Vol. 47, No. 1 Communications of the ACM – By Anil K Kain and Arun Ross Pg 37-38. http://www.csee.wvu.edu/~ross/pubs/RossMultibiometric_CACM04.pdf
4. Score normalization in multimodal biometric systems - Anil Jaina, Karthik Nandakumara, Arun Rossb, A. Jain et al. / Pattern Recognition 38 (2005) Pg 2270. http://biometrics.cse.msu.edu/Publications/Multibiometrics/JainNandakumarRoss_ScoreNormalization_PR05.pdf
5. Large-Scale Evaluation of Multimodal Biometric Authentication Using State-of-the-Art Systems - IEEE TRANSACTIONS ON PATTERN ANALYSIS AND MACHINE INTELLIGENCE, VOL. 27, NO. 3, MARCH 2005 - Robert Snelick, Pages 2-3. http://ieeexplore.ieee.org/iel5/34/30209/01388269.pdf
6. Multimodal Biometric Systems: A Survey - Arpit Gattani Utah State University – PDF Document – Pages 6. http://cc.usu.edu/~gattani/Biometrics-Gattani.doc
7. Score normalization in multimodal biometric systems - Anil Jaina, Karthik Nandakumara, Arun Rossb - Pattern Recognition 38 (2005) 2270 – 2285.
8. http://www.itl.nist.gov/iad/ 894.03/biometricscores/
9. http://www.neurotechnologija.com/mm_sdk.html
10. http://www.acsysbiometrics.com/product_sdk.html

11. Improving Personal Identification Accuracy Using Multisensor Fusion for Building Access Control Applications - Lisa Osadciw, Pramod Varshney, and Kalyan Veeramachaneni PG 1-2. http://ieeexplore.ieee.org/Xplore/login.jsp?url=/iel5/7951/2195 4/01020946.pdf
12. Validating a Biometric Authentication System: Sample Size Requirements – PDF document - Sarat C. Dass, Member, IEEE, Yongfang Zhu.. http://www.stt.msu.edu/~sdass/papers/DassZhuJain_SampleSize_PAMI06.pdf

BASE: a Proposed Secure Biometric Authentication System

Colby G. Crossingham and Sebastian H. von Solms

Academy For Information Technology
University of Johannesburg
Johannesburg, South Africa

Abstract. The use of biometrics as a secure remote authentication mechanism is hindered by a series of issues. In the case of fingerprints, an attacker can make physical copies of fingerprints by 'lifting' latent fingerprints off a non-porous surface. These lifted fingerprints can be used to illegitimately gain access to an authentication system. Password authentication systems only accept passwords that match 100%, whereas biometric authentication systems match submitted tokens provided they fall within a specified threshold. Without making use of a sufficient encryption scheme, illegitimately replaying a biometric token that has been tweaked slightly could still cause the authentication system to accept the submitted biometric token as a fresh biometric. BASE (Biometric Authentication System Entity), the proposed system, provides a solution to these challenges. As an alternative to current remote authentication systems, the BASE system utilizes a communication protocol that does not make use of encryption, passwords or timestamps, whilst still maintaining the security of the remote authentication process.

1   Introduction

Passwords have long been used as the mainstream mechanism for authentication. Even though there is a widespread popularity with using passwords, it is not difficult to recognize how vulnerable they are. In many cases passwords are forgotten, guessed, written down and even cracked using various brute-force attack techniques [1-3]. The need for more secure authentication mechanisms should be an important concern.In this paper, we are presenting the case of a large automotive- extended enterprise that decided to take action and takes care of its dealers network that are external actors interacting directly with the customers of the EE. We first present a literature review to clarify the reasons behind the importance of partnering with external actors for new product development and innovation, then we describe the CKN among the EE and its dealers´ network, and finally we discuss the organizational, technological and strategic dimensions of these interactions presenting some challenges facing the CKN and also especially some important factors that leads to success which is the creation, sharing and integration of knowledge in the new product development process of the extended enterprise.

Please use the following format when citing this chapter:

Crossingham, C. G. and von Solms, S. H., 2008, in IFIP International Federation for Information Processing, Volume 261; *Policies and Research in Identity Management*; Eds. E. de Leeuw, Fischer-Hübner, S., Tseng, J., Borking, J.; (Boston: Springer), pp. 91–102.

The problems associated with passwords have led to the option of using biometrics as a secure authentication mechanism instead. In the case of passwords, you cannot guarantee that the person in possession of the password is the authentic owner. The inherent property of biometrics is that only the authentic owner can produce them. Biometric authentication does not require a user to remember anything, nor be burdened with the responsibility of creating a strong password [3, 4]. There is even a wide array of biometric types to choose from, such as fingerprint, iris, voice and facial geometry.

After considering the many advantages of biometrics, the disadvantages are just as plentiful. Should a biometric ever be compromised in anyway, it is not possible to change it, as you could a password. In addition, passwords can be kept secret, but a biometric is constantly being exposed to the outside world. With fingerprints, every time a person touches a surface, a latent fingerprint can be left behind. This fingerprint can be 'lifted' and be transformed into a latex copy [2]. An attacker with this latex copy can then masquerade as the authentic owner.

Furthermore, if one wanted to create an online biometric authentication server that could authenticate thousands of users simultaneously whilst making use of an adequate encryption scheme, the processing overhead should be considered. A biometric in electronic form is generally much larger than a conventional password. To transfer biometric data securely across the Internet using Public Key Encryption (PKE) requires substantial startup overhead for the client and the server, as well as significant processing abilities on the server. Without making use of PKE, BASE can also avoid the possible weaknesses associated with cryptographic protocols [5].

Although some people view biometrics as an intrusive technology, this paper is focused on the technological elements associated with secure remote biometric authentication, and not on people-related issues associated biometric technology.

This paper presents a prototype system that has been developed to securely authenticate clients based on their biometrics, across an insecure network (such as the Internet), without making use of encryption, passwords or timestamping techniques [6, 7]. This prototype system, known as BASE, is presented in this paper as an alternative solution to current biometric authentication systems. BASE solves the problem of lifted fingerprints, replay attacks, server spoofing and numerous other less significant threats.

2 Design

Although BASE is a prototype system, it has been developed to closely replicate the role it would have if it were being deployed in the real world. The potential applications for a secure remote biometric authentication system are endless, so BASE has been developed with a framework that can cater for multiple clients in a variety of situations.

2.1   Biometric Types

The primary biometric used in developing and testing this prototype system has been fingerprints. Fingerprints are among the most common form of biometrics being used and they are also one of the easiest biometrics to replicate. It was important to develop and test the BASE system with a biometric such as fingerprints to overcome the issue of 'lifted' fingerprints.

The BASE system is by no means limited to one specific biometric type. The core framework and protocol remains identical regardless of what type of biometric token is being authenticated. Only the matching algorithm used on the BASE server needs to be changed depending on the biometric being authenticated.

2.2   System Framework

The BASE system has been designed to allow for a variety of authentication scenarios without changing the framework. For this reason, the BASE server has been implemented as a Web Service. Web Services allow multiple clients operating on different platforms, to make use of the same service. A second advantage to using Web Services is that it can be used in most cases without adding additional rules to client or server firewalls. Web Services use SOAP, an XML-based message protocol. The transport protocols that are commonly used to transmit the XML-based messages are HTTP and HTTPS, both of which are not normally filtered by network firewalls.

The BASE server operates using a database, which manages each client's account. Each client has an associated account on the BASE server to store client information.

2.3   Potential Applications

Although BASE is not restricted to any specific environment, the architecture of the prototype is primarily built to provide authentication from remote locations. By this it is meant that the BASE client and BASE server communicate with each other over an insecure network, from separate physical locations.

This type of authentication can be particularly beneficial in electronic commerce environments. Clients could do their shopping online, and securely authenticate themselves using their biometric, after which they would be charged for their purchases. In these scenarios BASE can be used to enforce non-repudiation, since it can be guaranteed that the biometric is originating from the authentic owner. During an e-commerce transaction, the BASE authentication server will act as a transaction facilitator between a merchant, an electronic cash broker and a client.

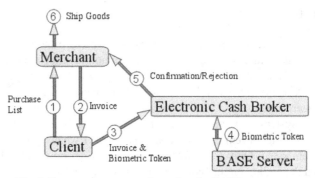

Fig. 1. E-commerce transaction using the BASE system.

The steps in Figure 1 above are as follows:

1. The client makes a selection of goods to purchase. The purchase list is sent to the merchant.
2. The merchant creates an invoice based on the client's purchase list. The merchant may chose to used encryption for transmitting the invoice, but this is not managed by the BASE system. The invoice is now sent to the client.
3. The client scans in his/her fingerprint, which is used by the BASE client application to create an authentication request (AR) message. The AR message is transmitted to the electronic cash broker, along with the invoice.
4. The electronic cash broker sends the AR message to the BASE server, to be authenticated. If the BASE server accepts the biometric, the electronic cash broker processes the invoice and makes the necessary cash transfers.
5. The merchant is now notified of the successful transaction.

In Figure 1, one should note that this scenario has been provided as a guideline for using BASE in an electronic commerce environment. It is possible to reorganize the entities involved in such an environment, so long as the biometric data generated by the BASE client, is transferred to the BASE server.

Because of the techniques used by the BASE system, if any illegitimate changes are made to the client's authentication request (AR) message at any stage, the BASE system will detect the change and reject the biometric.

2.4   Authentication Prerequisites

In order for clients to utilize the BASE system, they first need to be registered in the system. The registration process requires the client to physically travel to the institution making use of BASE technologies and scan their fingerprint. This scanned fingerprint is used as the registration template to authenticate the client during system operation.

After the registration template has been stored on the BASE server, the client is issued with a USB storage device. It is important to note that the content of the USB device should be inaccessible to anyone trying to access the data on it. A specific framework can be fused into the USB device to allow the device to act as a black box. An executable running on the USB device acts as the interface between the BASE client and the BASE server. The content on each USB storage device is specific to each client, and will be discussed in detail further in this paper.

The hardware protection of the USB storage device is beyond the scope of this paper. However, one recommendation is that a smart card can be used instead of a USB storage device, since smart cards have the ability to secure vital information located on the card.

3 Objectives

As previously mentioned, it was undesirable to make use of any encryption, passwords or timestamps during the transmission of biometric tokens. As a result the BASE system became vulnerable to a variety of attacks. Given that the intention of this prototype system was to introduce a different approach to secure authentication, these issues were solved without introducing encryption.

To facilitate secure biometric authentication, the BASE system identifies and prevents 4 main types of attack:

1. Simple replay attacks.
2. Tweaked token replay attacks.
3. Server spoofing attacks.
4. Lifted or copied biometrics.

3.1 Simple Replay Attacks

Every time the same client scans his/her fingerprint into a computer, it produces a different data stream. The chance of two fingerprint tokens from the same finger being exactly alike is almost impossible. Factors such as lighting, positioning and orientation of the finger, dirt and pressure can cause each scanned image to have subtle changes. These changes are reflected in the data stream transmitted to the server for authentication. The matching algorithm on the server is able to accept a biometric token provided it falls within an accepted threshold.

If an attacker intercepts an unprotected biometric token during transmission and replays the same biometric token at a later stage, it is easy to detect this simple replay attack. If the authentication server maintains an archive of previously accepted biometric tokens, and given the fact that no two biometric tokens should be the same, the authentication server can easily detect a simply replay attack if it receives a biometric token that has been sent before.

3.2   Tweaked Token Replay Attacks

In a password authentication system, the server only authenticates a user if the submitted password matches 100% to the stored original. This is known as symmetric matching. Biometric authentication works differently since no biometric token is the same. Biometric authentication uses asymmetric matching to determine if a biometric falls within an accepted threshold. This threshold will be configured on the server, when the BASE system is installed.

If an attacker intercepts a biometric token and tweaks the data slightly by changing a single byte and replays it, the server could accept it. The authentication server will see the submitted biometric token as a fresh token, since no record of it will exist in the archives. At this point the tweaked biometric token will be passed to the matching algorithm and could be authenticated, provided the token still falls within the accepted threshold.

3.3   Server Spoofing Attacks

PKE makes use of public/private key pairs that can be used to prove the authenticity of either the client or the server. Since BASE does not make use of PKE, it would be vulnerable to server spoofing attacks.

A client wishing to be authenticated could be deceived into sending a fresh biometric token to an attacker masquerading as the authentication server. The attacker could then send the 'stolen' biometric token to the authentic server to be authenticated. The authentication server would then illegitimately authenticate the attacker, since the biometric token being sent would not exist in the server archive and it would pass the matching algorithm check.

3.4   Lifted or Copied Biometrics

Fingerprints are particularly vulnerable to being lifted and have copies made from them. Currently it is very difficult or even impossible for an attacker to obtain other forms of biometric without the owner's cooperation, but in due time this may not be the case. The problem of lifted or copied biometrics is currently an important one, especially when using fingerprints for authentication, as in the BASE prototype system.

An attacker in possession of a copy of a client's fingerprint can easily be illegitimately authenticated. The authentication server would accept the submitted biometric token as a fresh token, and the token would also pass the matching algorithm check since it originated from the legitimate owner.

4 Implementation

In this section all the technical aspects of BASE are explained, as well as the communication that takes place between the client and server during authentication. As previously mentioned, a client needs to be registered in the BASE system before any authentication can take place. The registration process consists of three steps:

1. The client scans his/her fingerprint, producing a registration template. The registration template is stored on the server and used during authentication, for matching.

2. A Personal Token Archive (PTA) is created. A PTA is an archive consisting of space for 100 biometric tokens. During the registration process, the PTA is initialized to 100 randomly generated byte streams in equal length to a biometric token byte stream. The random byte streams in the PTA will slowly be replaced by biometric tokens during system operation. The reason for setting the size of the PTA to 100, is discussed in further detail in section 5.5.

    The PTA is copied to the client USB storage device and a copy of the PTA is stored on the BASE server. The associated token archive on the BASE server is referred to as the Master Token Archive (MTA).

3. A randomly generated key is created, referred to as the shared-key. The shared-key can be thought of as a serial number that is unique to each user. After the creation of the shared-key, it is copied to the client USB storage device and a copy is stored on the BASE server. The client never needs to be aware of the shared-key nor the PTA.

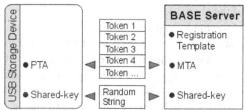

Fig. 2. Contents of the client USB storage device.

After the client has been registered in the system they are ready to make use of the BASE system for authentication. To be authenticated a client will need to insert their USB device into a machine, followed by scanning their fingerprint. The authentication process will follow.

4.1 Challenge Response Message

At the point where BASE clients need to be authenticated by the BASE server, they insert their USB storage device into a computer. A client executable located on the USB device executes, providing the client with an interface instructing him or her to place their fingerprint on the scanner. The biometric token produced from this scan is referred to as the fresh biometric token. Once the client has produced the fresh biometric token, the following operations are handled by the client executable.

Firstly, the client executable requests a Challenge Response (CR) message from the BASE server. This can be thought of as a handshaking process. To request the CR message from the server, the client generates a random string and passes it as parameters to the web service method, GenerateChallengeToken, along with the client's user name.

```
Client >> [GenerateChallengeToken(user_name, random_string)] >> Server
```

Upon arrival of the CR message request, the BASE server randomly selects a token in the MTA (a random number between 1 and 100). This selected token is known as the Challenge Token.

The BASE server now computes three MD5 hashes:
- The hash of the index of the Challenge Token.
- The hash of the random_string received by the client.
- The hash of the shared-key.

All of the above three hashes are XOR-ed with each other to produce the CR Message. The CR message is then returned to the client.

```
                    Server >> [CR Message] >> Client
```

4.2   The Authentication Request Message

Once the client has received the CR message from the BASE server, the Challenge Token index needs to be extracted. To begin breaking down the CR message the client computes two hashes:
- The hash of the shared-key
- The hash of the random_string

These two hashes are XOR-ed with each other to produce the CR key. The CR key is then XOR-ed with the CR message. The resulting product of the XOR is the hash of the index of the Challenge Token. Finally, to determine what number the remaining hash represents, the client does a quick brute force attack with numbers 1 to 100 (since 100 is the size of the MTA and PTA). Once the client finds a match to the hashed number, the client is aware of the Challenge Token.

An Authentication Request (AR) Message now needs to be created by the client to send to the server. The AR message is used to authenticate the client and is made up of three parts:
- A.   The user name associated with the client.
- B.   The fresh biometric that was scanned in by the client is XOR-ed with the Challenge Token located in the PTA, requested by the BASE server.
- C.   The MD5 hash of the fresh biometric token is XOR-ed with the hash of the shared-key.

4.3   Authentication

The BASE server will receive the AR message from the client, and based on the legitimacy of the contents, the server can either authenticate or reject the client request.

Since the server is aware of what Challenge Token to expect, the fresh biometric can be extracted from part B of the AR message. This is done by XOR-ing the expected Challenge Token in the MTA with part B of the AR message.

Secondly, since the server is also aware of the shared-key, the hash of the fresh biometric can be extracted from part C of the AR message.

The fresh biometric from part B of the AR message is hashed and compared to the extracted hash contained in part C of the AR message. If the hashes don't match the client is rejected, if not, the server continues onto the last step.

The final step in authenticating the client would be passing the extracted fresh biometric token to the matching algorithm. Based on the results of the matching algorithm, the client is either accepted or reject. If the client is accepted, the BASE server replaces the Challenge Token in the MTA with the extracted fresh biometric token. The client is then notified of the outcome of the authentication in the Server Response (SR) message.

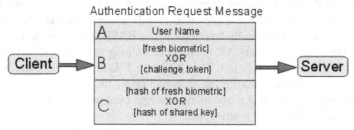

Fig. 3. The Authentication Request Message.

4.4   Server Response Message

The BASE server sends a clear text message indicating the success or failure of the authentication. No information needs to be protected in the SR message.

The client receives the server response message to determine whether or not the authentication was a success or not. If the client was authenticated successfully, then the Challenge Token in the PTA is replaced with the fresh biometric token that was used for authentication. After every successful authentication, the fresh biometric token replaces the Challenge Token in the PTA and MTA.

5 Evaluation

With the details of the BASE system explained, it will now be shown how each of the attacks previously identified are prevented by the BASE system. The four attacks identified were:
1. Simple replay attacks
2. Tweaked token replay attacks.
3. Server spoofing attacks.
4. Lifted or copied biometrics.
5. Hardware sniffing attack.

5.1   Simple Replay Attacks

Every time a client wishes to be authenticated, they first need to invoke the GenerateChallengeToken method on the BASE server. The server then returns the CR message containing the index of a specific Challenge Token to be used in the following AR message.

To initiate an authentication process, an attacker would first need to request a CR message. Since the attacker is not in possession of the shared-key, it is impossible to decipher the CR message. Should the attacker still attempt to replay the intercepted AR message, it will automatically be rejected. The BASE system never uses the same Challenge Token twice, so any AR message containing the wrong Challenge Token will cause the authentication to fail. The Challenge Token mechanism can be thought of as a one-time pad used during the construction of the AR message. The BASE system does not need to make use of timestamps because a replay attack will fail regardless of when the attack is attempted.

5.2   Tweaked Token Replay Attacks

In the case where an attacker attempts to tweak some part of an intercepted AR message and replay it, it will cause the BASE system to reject the AR message. The hash mechanisms contained within the AR message guarantee that the biometric data being sent has not been corrupted or tweaked in any way. The hash mechanisms used, inadvertently prevent AR messages with the wrong Challenge Token from being accepted.

5.3   Server Spoofing Attacks

The Challenge Response (CR) message requested from a client is used to prove the authenticity of the BASE server. An attacker spoofing the authentication server will not be able to produce a legitimate CR message because they are not in possession of the shared-key. If an attacker attempted to guess the shared-key, the CR message produced would make the Challenge Token index undeterminable by the client.

5.4   Lifted or Copied Biometrics

An attacker without the possession of a client's USB storage device would be unable to produce any legitimate AR messages. Every USB device contains a PTA and a shared-key, both of which are vital in deciphering the CR message and producing the appropriate AR message for authentication. Each USB device is specific to each client, so if an attacker used a lifted biometric with the wrong USB device, the system will reject the biometric token.

5.5   Hardware sniffing attack

During an authentication process, the client uses a fingerprint scanner to scan in their biometric. It is possible for an attacker to have port-sniffing software or hardware [8] to capture this fresh fingerprint data before it is even used by the BASE program. All fresh fingerprints are eventually placed in the PTA and MTA, and utilized in future authentication processes. Now, since the attacker has essentially obtained a PTA token (the sniffed fresh fingerprint from a previous authentication), they can construct an AR message by using a lifted fingerprint. The BASE system however, requires a random PTA token (the Challenge Token) to be used in each authentication process. For this type of attack to work, the attacker would need to use his/her sniffed token at exactly the right time. If an attacker submits his/her stolen token at the wrong time, BASE automatically detects this attack, and disables the client account. By increasing the size of the PTA and MTA from 100 to any larger number, reduces the chance of an attacker from using their stolen token at exactly the right time. Unfortunately, increasing the PTA and MTA size would also require more storage space on the server. The balance of security versus storage space must be decided on when setting up the BASE system.

6   Conclusion

The BASE prototype system has been developed and tested using the above attack scenarios. The system succeeds in preventing all of the attacks mentioned.

Due to the fact that the primary operation used by BASE is XOR, the system has extremely low processing overhead. Some cryptographic methods are used, but not PKE, thus the BASE system isn't affected by the problems associated with different encryption algorithms. The prototype system is also able to distinguish between false acceptance (legitimate rejections) and any form of attack. Since this is the case, BASE can stop multiple attack attempts after the first attempt without the need for an attempts counter [9].

If the BASE system were deployed for actual use, the client USB storage devices could be replaced by hardware protected smart cards or any device able to store and protect local data. The protection of the content on the client storage device is critical for the integrity of the system, but not considered apart of the scope of this paper.

Other biometric authentication systems exist [6, 10], however they make use of passwords, timestamps and public key cryptography to enforce security. The described BASE system may not be the only system that provides secure remote biometric authentication, but rather proposes an alternative solution with numerous benefits.

References

1. Halevi, S. and H. Krawczyk, Public-key cryptography and password protocols. ACM Transactions on Information and System Security (TISSEC), 1999. 2(3): p. 230-268.
2. Sukhai, N.B., Access control & biometrics. Information Security Curriculum Development, 2004: p. 124-127.
3. Tari, F., A.A. Ozok, and S.H. Holden, A comparison of perceived and real shoulder-surfing risks between alphanumeric and graphical passwords. ACM International Conference Proceeding Series, 2006. 149: p. 56-66.
4. Gupta, P., et al. Architectures for cryptography and security applications: Efficient fingerprint-based user authentication for embedded systems. in Proceedings of the 42nd annual conference on Design automation DAC '05. 2005.
5. Xu, S., G. Zhang, and H. Zhu, On the Properties of Cryptographic Protocols and the Weaknesses of BAN-like logics. ACM SIGOPS Operating Systems Review, 1997. 31(4): p. 12-23.
6. Khan, M.K. and J. Zhang, Improving the security of 'a flexible biometrics remote user authentication scheme'. Computer Standards & Interfaces, 2007. 29(1): p. 82-85.
7. Kim, H.S., S.W. Lee, and K.Y. Yoo, ID-based password authentication scheme using smart cards and fingerprints. ACM SIGOPS Operating Systems Review, 2003. 37(4): p. 32-41.
8. Roberts, C., Biometric attack vectors and defences. Computers & Security, 2007. 26(1): p. 14-25.
9. Ding, Y. and P. Horster, Undetectable on-line password guessing attacks. ACM SIGOPS Operating Systems Review, 1995. 29(4): p. 77-86.
10. Lin, C.-H. and Y.-Y. Lai, A flexible biometrics remote user authentication scheme. Computer Standards & Interfaces, 2004. 27(1): p. 19-23.

Identity and Privacy Protection

Are State-Mediated Forms of Identification a Reaction to Physical Mobility?

The case of England, 1500-2007

Edward Higgs

University of Essex, UK
ejhiggs@essex.ac.uk

Abstract. The development of technologies of identification has been linked to mobility, urbanisation and anonymity in both past and contemporary societies. This paper looks at England over the past 500 years to see if the history of mobility, urbanisation and identification mesh chronologically. Looking at the legal person, the citizen and the criminal deviant in turn, it argues that only in the case of the latter does there seem to be such a relationship. Even here, however, there appear to be other factors at work as well. Rather than mobility *per se* as the causal factor, the development of forms of identification seems to be linked to the changing relationships between individuals, commercial organisation and the state.

1 Introduction

The identification of individuals is an issue that increasingly preoccupies governments and inter-governmental organisations across the world. In the aftermath of 9/11, an ability to identify people crossing national boundaries is a top priority for the international political community. The International Civil Aviation Organization, for example, has sought to introduce machine-readable biometrics into all passports used for international travel [34, pp. 49-51]. Internally, states seem obsessed with pinning people down administratively to prevent terrorism, benefit fraud, and identity theft, which threaten states, welfare systems and markets alike. In Britain this has led to the passage of the 2006 Identity Cards Act, which authorises the issuing of identity cards to all British citizens and others resident in the country. These are also to contain biometric information and, according to the British Home Office, are intended to:

- help protect people from identity fraud and theft;
- ensure that people are who they say they are;
- tackle illegal working and immigration abuse;
- disrupt the use of false and multiple identities by criminals and those involved in terrorist activity;
- ensure free public services are only used by those entitled to them;

Please use the following format when citing this chapter:

Higgs, E., 2008, in IFIP International Federation for Information Processing, Volume 261; *Policies and Research in Identity Management*; Eds. E. de Leeuw, Fischer-Hübner, S., Tseng, J., Borking, J.; (Boston: Springer), pp. 105–120.

- enable easier access to public services [26].

Such developments are associated with an extensive raft of new identification technologies - DNA profiling, iris scanning, facial recognition systems, and so on.

The official drive to create foolproof means of identification has led to much public debate, and has been opposed by groups such as Liberty, the British civil liberties NGO [32]. In Britain, however, these public controversies have lacked, on the whole, an historical dimension. If identification is discussed in historical terms at all, media commentators usually go back no further than the national registration system of the Second World War [3]. Academic historians are, however, beginning to push back the history of identification into previous periods. One might include here Jane Caplan and John Torpey's excellent collection, *Documenting Individual Identity* [6], and Simon Cole and Chandak Sengupta's works on the introduction of fingerprinting in criminal forensics in the late nineteenth and early twentieth centuries [11; 48]. Sociologists, such as David Lyon in his *The Electronic Eye*, also attempt to place the surveillance of society in a temporal framework [35]. There are, in addition, a number historical works in which personal identification plays an incidental, but important, part, as in the recent biographies of impostors such as Perkin Warbeck and the Tichborne Claimant, and in Natalie Zemon Davis's *The Return of Martin Guerre* [64;38;13].[1] However, these works do not try to explain how differing forms of identification have developed over time, but rather how identification failed in particular cases of imposture.

In many of these works there is a tendency to understand the development of identification in terms the impact of increased mobility, consequent upon processes of industrialisation, which are associated with urbanisation and increasing social anonymity. This is most clearly seen in Cole's *Suspect Identities*, in which he argues that:

> In general, premodern societies already had an effective method of personal, and criminal, identification: the network of personal acquaintance through which persons were "known" in the memories and perceptions of their neighbors. Most people spent virtually their entire lives in the village, or region, in which they were born. ... In village society, there was little need for a signature to verify the identity of a neighbour. If a signature was used, it was more a gesture of good faith than a test of identity. ... In the wake of the industrial revolution, enormous numbers of people migrated from intimate rural villages to anonymous urban settings. Cities grew dramatically along with population density. The informal system of personal acquaintance and collective memory began to collapse [11, p.8].

Hence, Cole argues, the need for new forms of identification, such as the fingerprint, to deal with the rise of anonymity in society. Similarly, Sengupta in his

---

[1] Perkin Warbeck claimed to be one of the 'Princes in the Tower' murdered by their uncle, Richard III, who raised rebellions against Henry VII. The Tichborne Claimant was an impostor who claimed to be the heir to an English aristocratic estate in the mid-nineteenth century. The case of Martin Guerre involved the trial of a man who had pretended to be a French soldier returned from the wars in sixteenth-century France.

Imprint of the Raj, argues that fingerprinting can be seen within a context of urbanization and movement:

> Nineteenth-century Europe was a haven for criminals. Life was becoming steadily more urban, anonymous and mobile – in the large cities, one could simply disappear into a milling crowd of individuals and take on new identities that the surveillance and policing methods of the time could not hope to detect [48, p.9].

Even Caplan and Torpey, who are fully aware of the complexity of this history, see the development of identification in the period of the French Revolution and its aftermath against 'the background of an increasingly mobile society in which older and more stable conventions of identification were dissolving...' [6, p.7].

Many of these arguments draw, in part, on classical sociological concepts, especially those found in Ferdinand Tönnies's *Gemeinschaft und Gesellschaft*. Originally published in 1887, this work contrasts the supposed communal life of the ancient rural community, the *gemeinschaft*, with forms of contractual association in modern urban society, the *gesellschaft*. In the *gemeinschaft* people supposedly work together, and are bound by ties of kinship, tradition and the common tilling of the soil. The *gemeinschaft* is an 'organic' entity in which feelings of love, habit and duty are said to combine to create harmony, and where individuals are known to each other personally. Conformity to established social conventions is maintained by the family, and by the habitual deference due to friends and neighbours. In the *gesellschaft*, or so Tönnies argues, all are strangers to each other, and people are orientated towards the fulfilment of personal goals and the making of money. In this form of society, others become mere tools to personal gain in a market economy. The state then acts as a means of keeping individuals from each other's throats, and enforces the rule of capitalists over the discontented working classes [55]. This concept of a 'society of strangers' is also found in the work of the early twentieth-century sociologist Georg Simmel [50]. The vision of a mobile, anonymous, society is plainly one in which official forms of identification become necessary to prevent fraud and to impose social control.

The discussions of political scientists with regard to the development of modern identification systems for tracking and limiting the movements of migrants and asylum seekers is similarly couched in terms of the mobility of contemporary global society. According to Didier Bigo contemporary techniques of identification – passports, visas, identity cards - are merely a form of rhetoric, an illusion to give the impression that the nation state still has control over population flows in an era of economic globalisation, and of supra-national political structures such as the European Union [5; 1]. Stephen Castles, Professor of Migration and Refugee Studies at the University of Oxford, has also linked migration, security and surveillance [7, pp. 271-6]. Similarly, the sociologist David Lyon believes that, 'Mobility creates a world of nomads and unsettled social arrangements, so it is not surprising that in transit areas, such as airports, surveillance practices are intense' [36, p.19].

2   Mobility, urbanisation and anonymity in England

The equation 'modernity=mobility=anonymity=identification' which is found in much of this literature seems a fairly commonsensical one. Certainly the scale of cross border movements today would appear to require some forms of control mechanisms, however imperfect. According to Didier Bigo, for example, in the late 1990s the European countries covered by the Schengen agreements (France, Germany, the Benelux countries, Spain and Portugal) experienced 1.7 billion border crossings each year [5, p.158]. But the question still needs to be asked as to whether this simple relationship can be shown to explain processes of change in the past, or the context of contemporary developments. To do this, the present paper looks at one European county, England, over the last 500 years to see if the development of forms of identification can be seen as meshing with the history of mobility, industrialisation, and urbanisation. As the birthplace of the Industrial Revolution, and one of the earliest urban societies, one might assume that this relationship would be close and early.

First, one needs to say something about mobility in England since the sixteenth century. Contrary to what one might assume, England in the early-modern period was not an immobile society. The work of historical demographers, especially those of the Cambridge Group for the Study of Population and Social Structure, has shown that village populations in the past were constantly changing. At Honiger in Suffolk, for example, of the 63 family names recorded in parish registers of baptisms, marriages and burials in the period 1600 to 1634, only two could still be found in the registers for 1700 to 1724. Just over half the population of Cogenhoe in Northamptonshire disappeared and were replaced between 1618 and 1628. Whilst at Clayworth in Nottinghamshire the turnover of population between 1676 and 1688 approached two-thirds, of which only one-third can be explained in terms of mortality. People were constantly moving in search of employment or of land in a nascent market economy [61, p.42]. Such turnovers of population can indeed be pushed back in England into the later medieval period [15, pp.14-15]. Such mobility may have been unusual in Europe in this period.

However, most of these movements were probably over fairly short distances, and varied by region, period and social class. Small landowners probably stayed put, whilst landless labourers moved to find jobs [60]. Moreover, once people had moved, they probably worked locally, since the development of the modern pattern of daily commuting between place of work and place of residence residence was a nineteenth-century phenomenon [49, 117-57].   But those that had property had still to communicate over time and space through their wills and credit arrangements. They needed to prove their identity on documents that may have been created locally but needed to be lodged in various courts or in the money markets, often in London [39, pp.95-119].   The idea that early-modern Englishmen relied on trust in their commercial relationships is belied by the extreme litigiousness of the period.

Much of this movement was, of course, within the countryside, since it was only in 1851 that population censuses showed a majority of people in England living in settlements of 10,000 and over.   However, there were certainly large urban conglomerates in England prior to that date. In 1600 England was less urbanised than the average for Europe as a whole but by 1800 it was the second most urbanised country, after the Netherlands. In the late eighteenth century, perhaps 70 per cent of the total urban growth in Europe as a whole was taking place in England [63, pp.258-9]. Much of this urban growth could be found in the cities of the industrialising North and Midlands. Liverpool is estimated to have roughly trebled in size in the first four decades of the eighteenth century, and then increased more than fivefold between then and the end of the century, when its population stood at 82,000. By the end of the nineteenth century it was a conurbation of half a million. Birmingham, the centre of the metal industries, increased four and a half times between 1675 and 1760, and then doubled again by 1801 to 71,000. It had reached half a million by 1901 [14,pp. 7-8; 12, pp.234-5].

But all these urban centres were overshadowed by London, which had a population of about half a million in 1700, nearly one million in 1800, and contained two and a half million people by the 1850s. Throughout this period, London was probably the largest city in the world [18, pp.330-34]. By 1901 the vast majority of English men and women lived in towns. This urban growth implied migration from the countryside since the high mortality of the cities meant that many could not sustain their own populations by endogenous births, never mind expand. Thus, according to E. A. Wrigley, in the later seventeenth century migration to London from the rest of the country alone absorbed about half of the total birth surplus outside the capital [62]. But these processes of urbanisation accelerated in the eighteenth and nineteenth centuries, and reached their peak in the period from 1850 to 1890 [31, p.5].

To this vast internal migration must be added the waves of foreign migration experienced by England in the nineteenth century. Much of the European emigrant population of the newly independent USA passed through British ports such as Liverpool and London. By 1842 nearly 200,000 people were emigrating to the USA via Liverpool, something like half of all migrants leaving Europe. Between 1830 and 1930 over nine million people sailed from Liverpool bound for a new life in the USA, Canada and Australia [33]. There were also huge movements of the Irish into Britain in the wake of the Potato Famine of the late 1840s. This migration led to the establishment of large immigrant populations in Britain, especially in British cities. According to the 1861 census, out of a population of 20 million, England and Wales contained 600,000 people born in Ireland, 169,000 born in Scotland, and 84,000 persons born in other countries, half the latter being in London [8, p.39]. Many of these would have had children born in England, so the ethnic immigrant population was in fact larger than these figures suggest.

In general terms, therefore, one might argue that population mobility has always been a feature of English society, although this probably accelerating in the eighteenth and nineteenth centuries with industrialisation and urbanisation. Similarly, although England only became a predominantly urban country in the nineteenth century, it had significant urban environments in the early-modern period. In this England was probably unique in Europe, and was a model that other European countries followed in the late nineteenth and twentieth centuries.

English cities were certainly seen as anonymous places in the Victorian period but it is difficult to see such anonymity as anything new. Henry Fielding, the novelist and playwright, was complaining of the slums of London in the 1750s that,

> Had they been intended for the very purpose of concealment, they could hardly have been better contrived. Upon such a view [London] appears as a fast wood or forest, in which a thief may harbour with great security as wild beasts do in the deserts of Africa or Arabia [27, p.25].

Such beliefs may explain why, with his brother John, Fielding set up the Bow Street Runners, one of the first official police forces in London. Similar complaints could be heard, of course, about the capital in the sixteenth century, as in Nicholas Harman's *A Caveat for Common Cursitors*. Harman, for example, describes in his book of 1567 the activities of a 'counterfeit crank' who posed as a impoverished and diseased beggar in one part of town but actually lived as a gentleman on his proceeds in another [47, pp.110-18]. Of course, such anonymity may have been class specific – the urban poor may have been anonymous to the middle and ruling classes but familiar to each other. In Paris, for example, at the end of the eighteenth century, which was somewhat smaller than London but still had a population of perhaps half a million, there appears to have been no problem in identifying dead bodies pulled out of the Seine. The kin and neighbours of the dead were willing to come forward to identify them in the local morgue [10].

3   Multiple personality in England

Given this pattern of mobility and urbanisation, one would have expected the development of identification technologies in England to have taken place earlier than elsewhere, to be concentrated in the late eighteenth and nineteenth centuries, and to be strongly linked to mechanisms for social control. But is this, in fact, the case? However, before attempting to answer this question it is necessary to ask *what* is being identified by identification techniques. Although identification has always been applied to a human organism that acts, thinks and is embodied as an entity, that organism can be the bearer of multiple 'personalities' that can be identified in differing ways. Thus, returning to the uses of the new British identity card outlined above by the British Home Office, one can identify three sorts of personality that identification is intended to address:

1. the legal person who can own and alienate property, and enter into market transactions;
2. the citizen, or at least the person with a right to claim state welfare benefits;
3. the deviant criminal or alien who is to be the subject of control.

None of these personalities are natural; they are the product of social conventions since civil and administrative law does not exist in a state of brute nature. The legal person and the citizen are constituted as personalities by social practices imbedded in social interactions. One is a legal person because one can go to court to defend one's rights to property, and one is a citizen because one can make claims that the state recognises. The legal person and the citizen do not even need to have a body, since the dead can bequeath property via wills, or pass on pension rights. The criminal and the alien are treated as if they do not have such personalities, and do not therefore have some of these rights, or cannot make these claims.

In England these types of personality have historically been identified in very different ways. The legal person has tended to be identified by what he or she possesses, can do, or knows – seals, signatures, or PIN numbers. The citizen has tended to be identified via the community in the form of recognition by kin and neighbours, or through proof of official or commercial interactions. Only the criminal, and to some extent the alien, has been identified via the body, through branding, photography, fingerprinting, DNA profiling, and the like. Legal persons and citizens claim their identity, or have others claim it for them, only the deviant has an identity imposed upon them. It is partly the collapsing of these distinctions in the new identity card proposals, and in CCTV and online surveillance, that has raised public disquiet. So, taking these personalities separately, does the chronology of the development of forms of identification associated with them match the pattern of mobility and urbanisation noted above?

4 The identification of the legal person in England

In the case of the legal person the answer to this question probably has to be in the negative. The seal, for example, developed in England as a means of identifying the will of the legal person in the early middle ages. In Edward the Confessor's reign (1042-1066) only the king is known to have had a seal for authenticating documents, whereas in Edward I's reign (1273-1307) even serfs were required by statute law to have one. In the twelfth and thirteenth centuries the signature, or sign manual, was not accepted by itself as a lawful symbol of authentication on a document unless the signatory was a Jew. A Christian was required to either sign with a cross, indicating that he was making a promise in the sight of Christ crucified, or more commonly he affixed to the document his *signum* in the form of a seal [9, p.2, 233].

However, by the 1677 Statute of Frauds contracts had to be written and signed to be legal. The passage of this Act may possibly reflect the difficulty of proving rights to property in land in London after the disastrous Great Fire of London in 1666 had burnt down much of the old City [Hamburger]. One might also enquire if the shift away from the heraldic imagery of the seal, embodying the concept of the family estate, towards the personal performance of the signature, was not part of a larger trend towards possessive individualism in the period [37]. But after this date there were almost no innovations in the forms of legal identification until the late twentieth century. Then the introduction of automatic machine tellers (AMT) in London in 1967 necessitated the use of the first personal identification number (PIN), derived from the army number of the AMT's inventor, John Shepherd-Barron [4]. This seems to have been part of a reaction on the part of commercial organisations to a shift in the class basis of their customers. It is difficult to argue, therefore, that innovation in the identification of the legal personality had much to do with increased mobility during the eighteenth and nineteenth century.

5 The identification of the citizen in England

Similarly, the identification of the citizen does not seem to have responded to this process. In terms of their rights, people tended in early-modern England to be recognised within their community. From the early sixteenth century, baptisms, marriages and burials had to be recorded in parish registers, giving bureaucratic form to the passage of the soul through the local Christian community [23, pp. 1-2]. This system was replaced in 1837 by the modern civil registration of births, marriages and deaths, but it was still the duty of next of kin or neighbours to report these events to the local civil registrar. The process generated a portable record of one's birth, the birth certificate, which became a means of identifying oneself. But this was still parasitic upon communal identification [44, pp.25-36]. Also, the original reason for introducing civil registration was not fear of personal mobility but of the insecurity of property rights under the old parochial system [23, pp.7-17]. Similarly, from the early middle ages onwards the bodies of persons found dead were identified in the coroner's court by the first person that came across them, the 'first finder' - usually a member of the family or a neighbour [28, pp.1-36].

This sense of local belonging was carried over into the Poor Law system established by various Acts of Parliament from the early sixteenth century onwards. In very simplistic terms, under these Acts each parish was tasked with looking after its own poor people, who were said to have a 'settlement' there. Parish overseers of the poor were responsible for raising a local tax, the 'poor rate', and for using this money to provide 'relief' to their neighbours who had fallen on bad times. The 'deserving poor' were identified through personal acquaintance.   People who wondered about without a settled place of residence, 'vagrants' or 'vagabonds', were subject to various draconian penalties, culminating in death by hanging [51]. This system did not prevent mobility because one could obtain a settlement via residency and employment in another parish for a particular period. To make certain of their position under the Poor Laws, the mobile poor could obtain a 'settlement certificate' from their parish of settlement, indicating their right to poor relief there, that they presented to the overseers in their new home. Such identity papers meant that the receiving parish was thus guaranteed that the incoming person could be sent back to their parish of settlement for relief [52, pp.98-105].

This highly localised sense of belonging remained the basis of rights to welfare throughout the nineteenth century. In the countryside overseers of the poor continued to provide poor relief to their neighbours in their homes into the twentieth century. In the urban conurbations the increasing lack of personal knowledge of the poor by Poor Law officials did not lead to new forms of identification but to the 'workhouse test'. Under the 1834 New Poor Law Act, 'out-relief' of the poor in their own homes was supposedly outlawed, and those receiving relief had to do so in workhouses – virtual prisons in which they were put to work. This was mainly ignored in the countryside but not in the towns, where the poor had to present themselves at the workhouse door to claim relief. The urban poor had to identify themselves by a physical application for relief, rather than through carrying a means of identification [52, pp.207-338]. Indeed, rather than expanding the use of the settlement certificate as a means of identification, their issue by local Poor Law authorities seems to have ceased in the early nineteenth century [K. D. M. Snell, personal communication, 27/6/2006]. Thus, the increased mobility of the population in this period does not appear to have led to the development of new forms of identification.

In the Edwardian period the Poor Laws began to be superseded by centrally paid welfare payments such as old age pensions and national insurance. The 1908 Old Age Pensions Act gave the elderly pensions of 1s to 5s per week, provided that they did not receive poor relief after 1 January 1908; had not been imprisoned for any offence, including drunkenness, during the ten years preceding their claim; were not aliens or the wives of aliens; and could satisfy the pension authorities that they had not been guilty of 'habitual failure to work according to his ability, opportunity, or need, for his own maintenance or that of his legal relatives'. In all, less than 500,000 people received the benefit [54, p.103]. The national insurance system established by the 1911 National Insurance Act paid out limited unemployment benefits, and was at first only open to a small number of trades such as shipbuilding, engineering and construction. These covered about 2.5 million workers, out of a total male labour force of slightly over 10 million. By design, such trades included almost no women; were skilled and well-organised and provided stability of personnel; did not, by custom, see men being put on short-time during a depression; and, it was hoped, were trades subject only to reasonable and predictable seasonal fluctuations. National insurance also offered sickness benefits and basic medical care to those earning less than a specified annual income but not to their families and dependants. The system was administered by centrally-registered approved societies - friendly societies, commercial insurance companies, and some trade unions [19, p. 53, 88] [59]. In the course of the twentieth century the payment of such benefits expanded into the modern Welfare State.

Although this new form of centralised welfare led to the creation of vast systems of centralised record keeping [24 , pp.118-23], this does not appear to have led to a shift in identification practices. The identity of claimants was still proven through their links with others in the locality. In order to determine the claims of old age pensioners the local pensions officer was advised to get references from former employers, and 'respectable people on whose word reliance can be placed'. They could fall back on local 'poor law officials, ministers of religion, clerks to the justices, petty session clerks, collectors of rates, police officials, shopkeepers, or officials connected with friendly and other provident societies or with trade unions' [40, p.30-1]. People claiming unemployment benefits had to be certified by their late employers [41]. Similarly, the dependents of soldiers with children claiming war pensions had to be certified by persons of rank who 'believe her to be the person she represents herself to be', that is, ministers of religion, magistrates, physicians or surgeons, officers of HM services, school headmasters, secretaries of friendly societies, postmasters/mistresses, or police officers [42]. By the late twentieth century benefit claimants had to provide a wide range of documents showing that they were enmeshed in networks of social and official relations – tax forms, driving licences, contracts of employment, payslips, invoices and the like. The birth certificate could be supplied as proof of identity but it was not the only document allowed.

New systems for the identification of citizens for welfare purposes were introduced in Britain during wartime. During both World Wars identification cards and certificates were issued to the population as part of national registration for conscription purposes. They were also used for rationing in the First and Second World Wars, and for the claiming benefits in the latter, and in its immediate aftermath. But the system was wound up in 1952, and not resurrected until the early twenty-first century [24, p.134-44]. Similarly, from time to time the concept of a benefit payment card has been mooted as a means of identification for welfare claimants but trials of these have come to nothing [43]. Once again, few of these developments seem to reveal a quantum leap in the forms of identification used by citizens as a consequence of increased mobility.

Similarly, the history of the international passport fails to show a close correspondence with population mobility. The passport has had a long history in Europe, going back to the late middle ages. However, during the nineteenth century people moved into and out of Britain with few restrictions, and the use of passports declined generally throughout Europe [21, pp.156-64, 235]. This system of *laissez faire* was not abandoned because of population mobility, rather it was a victim of democracy and the First World War. With the expansion of voting rights to the working population in the late nineteenth century, immigration, especially into the East End of London, became a political issue that right-wing politicians could mobilize in search of votes. The 1905 Aliens Act began the process of tightening up foreign immigration [16, pp.69-73, 170-98]. With the outbreak of war, the 1914 Aliens Restriction Act passed in August of that year, gave the government still greater powers to restrict such movement. This increasing sensitivity to perceived threats from abroad was shared by states across the developed world, and led to the creation of the modern system of international passports. The first modern United Kingdom passport was issued in 1915 when the 1914 Status of Aliens Act came into force. The new passport contained the personal description of the holder, giving the shape of the person's face, their features (nose: large, forehead: broad, eyes: small) as well as their complexion, a photograph, and their signature [57]. The wartime restrictions were extended after the period of conflict by the Aliens Order of 1920, that laid down that anyone wanting to enter or leave the country had to carry a passport indicating his or her nationality and identity. In a world in which citizens were being mobilised for total warfare, all foreign nationals became a potential threat [56]. What was important here was the nature of the relationship between the state and the citizen, rather than mobility *per se*.

6   The identification of the deviant in England

Given the importance attached to the identification of the deviant in the current historiography of identification, one might expect this facet of personal identification in England to reveal the closest meshing with increasing mobility and urbanization. To some extent this is the case. Certainly, the nineteenth century saw a number of innovations in forensic identification in England. Registers of distinctive marks began to be compiled by the new uniformed police forces set up in the period, supplemented by the development of the photographic 'mug shot' from the mid Victorian period onwards. A Habitual Criminals Registry was set up by the Metropolitan Police as a consequence of the 1869 Habitual Criminals Act that imposed extra punishments on repeat offenders. The Registry eventually came to introduce fingerprinting as the main form of criminal identification in the Edwardian period, after briefly experimenting with the 'anthropometric system'. The latter, developed by Alphonse Bertillon in Paris, involved recording the measurements of limbs and facial features of criminals. In the twentieth century such means of forensic identification were supplemented by serology, facial reconstruction, and, of course, DNA profiling [24, pp. 95-7, 113-18, 182-3].

Such developments can thus be placed in the context of the broad picture of mobility, urbanization and anonymity in England. However, the lack of any significant innovations in the eighteenth and early nineteenth centuries seems somewhat problematic given the Industrial Revolution of this period. There were also deep continuities. The criminal in England had always been identified via the body from the early-modern period onwards. Vagrants under the Old Poor Laws could be branded, whilst the physical descriptions of felons were circulated in newspapers, and on posters, from an early date [53]. The development of the criminal registry, and the capture of the likeness of the criminal, can be found in Europe in the medieval period [21,pp. 69-77]. Moreover, suggestions that such forms of physical identification should be extended to the legal person or the citizen were generally rejected in the English context until the recent passage of the Identity Cards Act.

There were also other forces at work here than a simple reaction to increasing mobility. It has been suggested, for example, that the moral panics over crime in the Victorian period did not represent a rational reaction to increasing crime levels, since the increasing number of criminal indictments merely reflected the increasing activities of the police [17]. What was more fundamentally at stake was the desire of the middle classes, who had won increased political power in the 1832 Reform Act, to control the 'criminal classes', especially in the aftermath of the French Revolution [46]. This can be seen as part of a much wider bourgeois attempt to infuse order into the urban landscape [29]. The passing of the Habitual Criminals Act can, in a sense, be seen as a result of the restriction of the mobility of criminals. It was the ending of the transportation of convicts to the Australian colonies that created the fear of a sedentary criminal class in England, and so prompted the creation of a more draconian penal system [25, cols. 332-45]. Similarly, the 1869 Habitual Criminals Act might be understood, in part, as a reaction to the passing of the 1867 Reform Act, which gave voting rights to many working-class men. The criminal could no longer be seen simply as a member of the lower orders, he or she had now to be reconceptualised as a degenerate sub-culture beyond the constitutional pale [58, pp. 300-6, 342-58]. One might even argue that criminality had to be raised to the level of a social pathology in order to justify the vast network of police and prisons in a liberal society [30, pp. 296-308].

Yet again, the origins of modern fingerprinting lay not in Britain's industrializing cities but in rural Hampshire and British India. In the late 1860s and early 1870s probably the most infamous man in Britain was the Tichborne Claimant, a butcher from Wagga Wagga in Australia who claimed to be Sir Roger Tichborne, the heir to the Tichborne estates in Hampshire, who had been lost at sea in 1854. The Claimant was eventually unmasked as an imposter but only after two inordinately long and costly court trials [2;38]. The cases involved a vast range of identification evidence – eye witness testimony, photographs, tattoos, hair samples, and even the size of the Claimant's penis – much of which was inconclusive. This attack on property rights led to a desire to discover a foolproof method of personal identification, and thus to the work of Sir Francis Galton on fingerprint identification. Galton, a redoubtable Victorian polymath, wrote extensively on the subject but his classification system for fingerprints was too cumbersome to be easily used in forensics [20, pp.231-49]. The classification which was eventually introduced into British police work in the early twentieth century came out of the experience of police work in British India. Given the British assumption that all Indians were dishonest, and could not be distinguished from each other, fingerprinting did represent a reaction to anonymity but in a particular racial and imperial context [48].

In sum, although there seems to be a *prima facie* correspondence between the history of mobility in England and forms of identification for criminals, the causal link becomes less apparent on closer inspection.

7   Towards a conclusion

Many aspects of the need for personal identification in the contemporary world are plainly linked to mobility. This is most obviously seen in the case of the tracking of international terrorists and criminals. However, an examination of the history of identification in England over the past 500 years shows that this has not always been the case. The developments in the identification of the legal person and the citizen do not appear to follow the chronology of changes in patterns of mobility. Indeed, in the nineteenth century, when mobility was increasing, there was little innovation in these fields, and, in some respects, a curtailment of identification practices. In the twentieth century the movements of citizens were controlled via the passport system but this represented a new relationship between the state and the citizen. States came to see citizens of other states as potential enemies in an age of total military mobilization, whilst their own citizens saw their citizenship as a patrimony that needed to be defended against immigrants. In the case of the identification of the criminal the chronologies do mesh more closely, although the absence of innovations in the eighteenth and early nineteenth centuries is problematic. Moreover, it is not always clear that changes in criminal identification in the late nineteenth and twentieth centuries can be seen simply in terms of mobility.

This, of course, raises the question as to why the British state has suddenly decided that the distinctions between the identification of legal persons, citizens and deviants needs to be effaced. Rather than seeing this simply as the cumulative effect of population mobility, urbanization and anonymity, one might have to look for changes in the relationship between the state and civil society. In England in the modern period the state has generally trusted civil society to go about its business unhindered. As long as citizens obeyed the law, and accepted the market economy, the party political system, and the territorial integrity of the United Kingdom, they were generally left to get on with their lives. Legal persons could be trusted to maintain their own forms of identification, and communities and social interactions could be used to prove the identity of welfare claimants. But relationship is now being undermined, possibly reflecting the decline in inter-personal trust that has been a general feature of Western society in the post-war period [45, pp.121-31]. The state no longer believes that civil society can be trusted with many facets of identification. This is a fundamental shift in the relationship between the government and the governed, and seems to have comparatively little to do with mobility *per se*.

References

1.   Malcolm Anderson, Didier Bigo, Ed Bort, 'Frontiers, identity and security in Europe, an agenda of research', in Martin Pratt and Janet Allison Brown (eds), *Borderlands Under Stress* (London: Kluwer Law International, 2000), pp. 251-74.

2.   Robyn Annear, *The Man Who Lost Himself. The Unbelievable Story of the Tichborne Claimant* (London: Robinson, 2002).

3.   BBC News Website 1: 'When the British fought off ID cards', http://news.bbc.co.uk/1/hi/magazine/3129302.stm (9/7/2007).

4.   BBC News Website 2: http://news.bbc.co.uk/1/hi/business/6230194.stm#toolbar (13/7/07).

5.   Didier Bigo, 'Frontiers and security in the European Union: the illusion of migration control', in Malcolm Anderson and Eberhard Bort (eds.), *The Frontiers of Europe* (London: Pinter, 1998), pp 148-64.

6.   Jane Caplan and John Torpey, *Documenting Individual Identity. The Development of State Practices in the Modern World* (Princeton: Princeton University Press, 2001).

7.   Stephen Castles and Mark J. Miller, *The Age of Migration* (Basingstoke: Palgrave Macmillan, 2003).

8.   Census of England and Wales, 1861, General report [Vol. III.], British Parliamentary Papers 1863 LIII (3221).

9.   M.T. Clanchy, *From Memory to Written Record: England 1066-1307* (Oxford: Blackwell Publishing, 1993).

10. Richard Cobb, *Death in Paris 1795-1801* (Oxford: OUP, 1978).

11. Simon Cole, *Suspect Identities. A History of Fingerprinting and Criminal Identification* (Cambridge, MA: Harvard University Press, 2001).

12. Chris Cook and Brendan Keith, *British Historical Facts 1830-1900* (New York; St Martin's Press, 1975).

13. Natalie Zemon Davis, *The Return of Martin Guerre* (Cambridge, MS: Harvard University Press, 1983).

14. Phyllis Deane and W. A. Cole, *British Economic Growth 1688-1959* (Cambridge: Cambridge University Press, 1969).

15. Christopher Dyer, 'Were late medieval English villages 'self-contained', in Christopher Dyer (ed.), *The self-contained village? The social history of rural communities 1250-1900* (Hatfield: University of Hertfordshire Press, 2007), pp. 6-27.

16. Bernard Gainer, *The alien invasion : the origins of the Aliens Act of 1905* (London : Heinemann Educational Books, 1972).

17. V. A. C. Gatrell and T. B. Hadden, 'Criminal statistics and their interpretation', in E. A. Wrigley (e.d) *Nineteenth-Century Society. Essays in the Use of Quantitative Methods for the Study of Social Data* (Cambridge: Cambridge University Press, 1972), pp. 336-396.

18. Robert Gray, *A History of London* (London: Hutchinson, 1978).

19. Bentley B. Gilbert, *British social policy 1914-1939* (London: B.T.Batsford, 1970).

20. Nicholas Wright Gillham, *A Life of Sir Francis Galton: from African Exploration to the Birth of Eugenics* (Oxford: Oxford University Press, 2001).

21. Valentin Groebner, *Who are you? Identification, deception and surveillance in early modern Europe* (Brooklyn, NY: Zone Books, 2007).

22. Philip Hamburger, 'The conveyancing purposes of the Statute of Frauds', *American Journal of Legal History*, 27 (1983), pp. 354-85.

23. Edward Higgs, *Life, Death and Statistics: Civil Registration, Censuses and the work of the General Register Office, 1837-1952*, (Hatfield, Local Population Studies, 2004).

24. Edward Higgs, *The Information State in England. The Central Collection of Information on Citizens since 1500* (Basingstoke: Palgrave Macmillan, 2004).

25. *Hansard's Parliamentary Debates*, 3rd series, Vol. CXCIV.

26. Home Office Website: http://www.homeoffice.gov.uk/passports-and-immigration/id-cards/why-we-need-id-cards/ (9/7/2007).

27. Robert Hughes, *The fatal shore. A history of the transportation of convicts to Australia, 1787-1868* (London: Guild Publishing, 1987).

28. R.F. Hunnisett, *The Medieval Coroner*, (Cambridge: Cambridge University Press, 1961).

29. Patrick Joyce, *The Rule of Freedom. Liberalism and the Modern City* (London: Verso, 2003).

30. Michel Foucault, *Discipline and Punish. The Birth of the Prison* (London: Allen Lane, 1977).

31. Eric E. Lampard, 'The urbanizing world', in H. J. Dyos and Michael Wolff (eds), *The Victorian City: Images and Realities, Volume I* (London: Routledge & Kegan Paul, 1976), pp. 3-58.

32. Liberty Website: http://www.liberty-human-rights.org.uk/issues/3-privacy/31-id-cards/index.shtml (9/7/2007).

33. Liverpool Maritime Archives & Library Sheet No. 64 : Liverpool and Emigration in the 19th and 20th Centuries http://www.liverpoolmuseums.org.uk/maritime/archive/displayGuide.aspx? (12/7/2007).

34. London School of Economics, *The Identity Project. An Assessment of the UK Identity Cards Bill and its Implications* (London: LSE, 2005).

35. David Lyon, *The Electronic Eye. The Rise of Surveillance Society* (Cambridge: Polity Press, 1994).

36. David Lyon, *Surveillance Society. Monitoring Everyday Life* (Buckingham: Open University Press, 2001).

37. C. B. Macpherson, *The Political Theory of Possessive Individualism. Hobbes to Locke* (Oxford: Clarendon Press, 1962).

38. Rohan McWilliam, *The Tichborne Claimant. A Victorian Sensation* (London: Hambledon Continuum, 2007).

39. Craig Muldrew, *The Economy of Obligation. The Culture of Credit and Social Relations in Early Modern England* (Basingstoke: Macmillan, 1998).

40. National Archives, London: Board of Inland Revenue and Board of Customs and Excise: Non Contributory Old Age Pensions, Registered Files (AST 15):AST 15/64 Old Age Pensions Acts 1908 and 1911: Instructions to Pension Officers; proofs 1911-1913.

41. National Archives, London: Ministry of Labour and successors: Circulars and Codes of Instructions (LAB 29): LAB 29/237 Instructions regarding investigations of claims 1936.

42. National Archives, London: Ministry of Pensions and successors: War Pensions, Registered Files (GEN Series) and other records (PIN 15): PIN 15/1352 Identification of Pensioners 1917-1923.

43. National Audit Office, The Cancellation of the Benefits Payment Card Project, http://www.nao.org.uk/publications/nao_reports/9900857.pdf.

44. Muriel Nissel, *People Count. A History of the General Register Office* (London: HMSO, 1987).

45. Avner Offer, *The Challenge of Affluence. Self-Control and Well-Being in the United States and Britain since 1950* (Oxford: Oxford University Press, 2006).

46. David Philips, ''A new engine of power and authority': the institutionalisation of law-enforcing in England 1780-1830', in V Gatrell, B Lenman, and G Parker (eds), *Crime and the law: the social history of crime in Western Europe since 1500* (1980), pp. 155-89.

47. Gamini Salgado (ed.), *Cony-Catchers and Bawdy Baskets* (Harmondsworth: Penguin, 1972).

48. Chandak Sengoopta, *Imprint of the Raj. How Fingerprinting was Born in Colonial India* (London: Macmillan, 2003).

49. Francis Sheppard, *London 1808-1870: the Infernal Wen* (London: Secker & Warburg, 1971).

50. George Simmel, *The Stranger* (Chicago: Chicago University Press, 1971).

51. Paul Slack, *Poverty and Policy in Tudor and Stuart England,* (London: Longman, 1988).

52. K. D. M. Snell, *Parish and Belonging. Community, Identity, and Welfare in England and Wales, 1700-1950* (Cambridge: Cambridge University Press, 2006).

53. John Styles, 'Print and policing: crime advertising in 18th century England', in Douglas Hay and Francis Snyder (eds), *Policing and prosecution in Britain 1750-1850* (Oxford: Clarendon Press, 1985), pp. 55-112.

54. Pat Thane, 'Non-contributory versus insurance pensions 1878-1908', in Pat Thane (ed.), *The origins of British social policy* (London: Croom Helm, 1978), pp. 84-106.

55. Ferdinand Tönnies, *Community and civil society (Gemeinschaft und Gesellschaft)* (Cambridge: CUP, 2001).

56. John Torpey, 'The Great War and the birth of the modern passport system', in Jane Caplan and John Torpey (eds), *Documenting individual identity.The development of state practices in the modern world* (Princeton: Princeton University Press, 2001), pp. 256-70.

57. UK Passport Service Website: http://www.ukpa.gov.uk/_history/history_03.htm (7 May 2002).

58. Martin J. Weiner, *Reconstructing the Criminal.Culture, Law, and Policy in England, 1830-1914* (Cambridge: Cambridge University Press, 1990).

59. Noel Whiteside, 'Private provision and public welfare: health insurance between the wars', in David Gladstone, *Before Beveridge. Welfare before the Welfare State* (London: IEA Health and Welfare Unit, 1999), pp. 26-42.

60. Jane Whittle, 'Population mobility in rural Norfolk among landowners and others c.1440-c.1600', in Christopher Dyer (ed.), *The self-contained village? The social history of rural communities 1250-1900* (Hatfield: University of Hertfordshire Press, 2007), pp. 28-45.

61. Keith Wrightson, *English Society, 1580-1680* (London: Routledge, 1993).

62. E. A. Wrigley, 'A simple model of London' s importance in changing English society and economy 1650-1750, *Past and Present* 37 (1967), pp. 44-70.

63. E. A. Wrigley, *Poverty, Progress and Population* (Cambridge: Cambridge University Press, 2004).

64. Ann Wroe, *Perkin. A Story of Deception* (London: Vintage, 2004).

Privacy Risk Perceptions and Privacy Protection Strategies

Isabelle Oomen and Ronald Leenes

TILT – Tilburg Institute for Law, Technology, and Society
Tilburg University, the Netherlands
r.e.leenes@uvt.nl

Abstract. Several opinion polls have reported that many people claim to be concerned about their privacy, yet that most people in fact do very little to protect their privacy. Are privacy concerns indeed insufficient motivators to adopt privacy protection strategies? What then characterizes the users of these strategies? On the basis of a large scale survey amongst Dutch students, this paper explores the relation between privacy risk perception and privacy protection strategies in more detail. It elaborates on factors that constitute privacy risk perception, as well as three kinds of strategies adopted by individuals to protect their privacy: behavioral measures, common privacy enhancing technologies (PETs), and more complex PETs. Next, it explores the relation between the respondents' perception and the strategies they employ in more detail to answer the question what characteristics the users of the various strategies have in terms of perception, gender and age. Gender appears not to influence privacy risk perception, yet men are more familiar with the various privacy protection strategies and use them more of-ten than women. In general, a higher privacy risk perception does not lead to the adoption of stronger or more protection strategies, except for the use of pseudonyms, cookie crunchers, anonymous email, safe email, and providing false personal data. Our analysis deepens the understanding of privacy risk perception and privacy protection strategies, yet leaves the privacy paradox unresolved.

1 Introduction

Many opinion polls report that although the overwhelming majority of people claim to be concerned about their privacy, most people in fact do very little to protect it[1]. This paradox is often explained by stating that people lack information, that they don't know the degree to which their information is being collected, and that they are unaware of the potentially harmful consequences of this practice (e.g., [14]). Most studies, however, don't explore the relationship between the privacy risk perception of individuals and their subsequent actions to protect their privacy in depth or in detail. Opinion polls go no further than to mention: X % claims to be concerned about their privacy and Y % says that they have taken action to protect their privacy. This raises

[1] For a list of opinion polls, see: http://www.epic.org/privacy/survey

Please use the following format when citing this chapter:

Oomen, I. and Leenes, R., 2008, in IFIP International Federation for Information Processing, Volume 261; *Policies and Research in Identity Management*; Eds. E. de Leeuw, Fischer-Hübner, S., Tseng, J., Borking, J.; (Boston: Springer), pp. 121–138.

the question: How are privacy risk perception and the actions people take to protect their privacy related to each other?

In this study, we explore this question in more detail on the basis of empirical research among Dutch students. We particularly focus on privacy risk perception, the strategies students employed to protect their privacy and the relation between the two. We also explore whether age and gender are related to privacy risk perceptions and adopted strategies.

2   From perception to action

Before cheap printed material was widely available, communication was mainly two-way, face to face. Printed material changed this. One-way communication gained importance with the effect that the identity of the other often is unknown, i.e. the author reveals without being revealed and the reader learns without being learned about. The current shift to electronic communication changed the communication back to two-way [14]. Electronic communication inevitably leaves traces which makes it possible for anybody interested enough to collect, organize, and analyze personal information of others [12]. It is increasingly difficult to reveal without being revealed and to learn without being learned about [14]. As the recognition of this phenomenon grows, privacy has increased in salience.

In the context of online behavior, informational privacy is at stake. Informational privacy relates to an individual's right to determine how, when, and to what extent information about herself will be released to others [1-2, 15]. The acquisition, storage, manipulation, mining, sharing, selling and analysis of personal data represent violations of the individual's informational privacy. It may also lead to practices like identity theft, social sorting, and far-going surveillance [8, 9-11, 13]. Privacy risks are regarded as the consequences of the abuse of misuse of personal information. Possible privacy risks can thus be identity theft, loss of freedom, threat to personal safety, threat to dignity, invasion of the private sphere, unjust treatment, or financial loss. The perception of these risks varies from individual to individual based on that person's own values and general perceptions, and her experiences [1, 6].

When people perceive risks, they want to reduce them. We distinguish three groups of strategies that individuals may employ to do so. The first group involves behavioral strategies. Providing incorrect answers when personal information is requested is a strategy that can be applied easily in online environments. Other examples are the use of anonymous email addresses and the use of pseudonyms. The second group comprises well known security measures and PETs. Spam filters, firewalls, and anti spyware have become standard PETs on almost every computer (that runs on a Microsoft platform). The third group of strategies consists of more advanced PETs. These are more difficult to implement and sometimes require cooperation of service providers which limits their use. Examples of these PETs are: encryption tools, anonymous remailers, trust certificates, anonymisers, cookie crunchers, password managers or vaults, and safe email. Because they are easier to implement, we assume that behavioral privacy protection strategies and common PETs are used more often than advanced PETs.

Hypothesis 1:   Behavioral privacy protection strategies and common PETs are used more often than advanced PETs.

People with a weak privacy risk perception will have less incentives to use privacy protection strategies and we expect these individuals therefore not to use them. Individuals with stronger privacy risk perceptions, on the other hand, are more likely to adopt one or more privacy protection strategies to counter or limit the risks. Conversely, we assume that people who use privacy protection strategies to have a stronger privacy risk perception (i.e. they perceive their privacy risk higher) than people who don't use these strategies. Because advanced PETs require extra effort (i.e. they are not pre-installed on computers and one has gain knowledge about their existence, get possession of them, and learn how to use them), it is likely that people who use these advanced PETs have a higher privacy risk perception – their concerns outweighs the required efforts – than people who only use common PETs or behavioral strategies.

Hypothesis 2:   Internet users who use privacy protection strategies have a stronger privacy risk perception than those who don't use these strategies.

Hypothesis 3:   Internet users who (also) use advanced PETs have a higher privacy risk perception than those who only use common PETs or behavioral strategies

The different strategies are, of course, not mutually exclusive. It is likely that the adoption of one strategy will reinforce the use of the other strategies. Therefore, we assume that there is a positive relationship between the use of strategies.

Hypothesis 4:   There are positive relationships between the various strategies.

Figure 1 shows the presumed relationships.

3   Measuring privacy risk perception and protection strategies

The data used for this paper is collected as part of the EU FP6 PRIME project[2]. The PRIME project aims to develop privacy-enhancing identity management tools. In order to gain a better understanding of user needs, large scale surveys are conducted among European internet users.

For the present study a sample of Dutch university and college students was chosen due to time and budget restraints. This approach limits the generalizations of the findings. Twenty six Dutch universities and colleges of further education where approached with a request to forward an email invitation to participate in the survey to their students. Five institutions, two universities and three colleges, forwarded our email invitation containing a link to the online questionnaire. Three universities and four colleges, either placed the message on their website or in their newsletter. As an

---

[2] See http://www.prime-project.eu for information about the project and its public deliverables.

incentive for the students to participate, four iPod nano's (2GB) were raffled among the respondents.

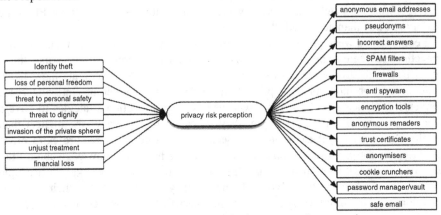

Fig. 1. Privacy risk perception and privacy protection strategies.

The survey ran from Friday December 15th 2006 until Tuesday January 9th 2007. In total, 5541 students participated in the online survey. The response rate for students invited by email was 6.43%, while the response rate for students invited by an announcement on the website or in the newsletter was 0.3%. The overall response rate was 2.31%.

The questionnaire addressed demographics of the respondents, their online activities, their trust with respect to public and private institutions, their general concerns, their concerns with respect to personal data and privacy, and their knowledge and experience with privacy enhancing technologies. The respondents were also randomly assigned to answer questions about one out of four specific online contexts: e-government, online shopping, online banking, and online travel booking. This resulted in a total of 295 variables, of which a few are used in the present study.

Completing the full questionnaire took approximately 30 minutes. Consequently, some 25% (1374) of the respondents did not complete the questionnaire. Respondents with more than 75% missing data were deleted from the sample set. The data of 5139 respondents was used for the analyses and the remaining missing data were handled by using list wise deletion in the analyses.

In the sample 52% of the respondents were male and 48% were female. University students amount for 60.7% of the sample against 39,3% for the colleges of higher education. Due to the participation of the Open University, with students of all ages, the distribution of age of the respondents showed a large variation. Most respondents (85%) are under 28, still 10% of the respondents is older than 32 and 5% of them is even older than 42, one of the students reported 72 years of age. The mean age in the sample was 24.2 (SD = 7.74).

4   Analyses[3] and results

We will first focus on the respondents' perception of specific privacy risks and the theoretical construct privacy risk perception. Next we address the use of privacy protecting strategies by the respondents and whether gender affects the use of different strategies. Finally, the privacy risk perceptions of the groups within the strategies were compared.

4.1   Privacy risk perception

Privacy risk perception of the respondents was measured by seven items on a five point scale as part of the question: 'How concerned are you in general about the following possible consequences of abuse/misuse of your personal information?' The concerns listed were: 'threat to your personal safety', 'loss of personal freedom', 'invasion of your private sphere', 'financial loss', 'possibility of identity theft', 'unjust treatment', and 'threat to you dignity'. The answers were: 'not at all' (1), 'barely' (2), 'neutral' (3), 'slightly' (4), and 'considerably' (5). The means of these items are displayed in table 1. The respondents are most concerned about invasion in their private sphere, with a mean of 3.42 (on a five point scale). They are least concerned about the possible threat to their dignity and about receiving an unjust treatment as a result of abuse or misuse of their personal data, with means of 2.84 and 2.85 respectively.

Table 1. Privacy risk perception.

	M (SD)	Privacy risk perception
Loss of freedom	3.07 (1.198)	.837
Threat to personal safety	2.92 (1.191)	.819
Threat to dignity	2.84 (1.186)	.814
Invasion of the private sphere	3.42 (1.137)	.805
Unjust treatment	2.85 (1.152)	.777
Possibility of identity theft	3.14 (1.223)	.773
Financial loss	3.17 (1.151)	.716
Mean	3.06	
Explained variance	63%	
α	.90	

Notes: N=4424

        Values are component loadings

        Method: Principal Component Analysis

Moderate to high, positive, and significant (Pearson product-moment) correlations were found between the items, ranging from .463 to .729 (not in the table). There are positive relationships between the specific privacy risk perceptions. This indicated that the items could represent a common concept. A principal component analysis was

---

[3] Performed with SPSS (v13.0 and v15.0), see [7]. For more information about the mathematics behind the analyses see, for example, [5].

conducted to test this assumption. One component was found, indicating that these seven items together measure the same latent construct: privacy risk perception. The component loadings in the second column of table 1 reflect the contribution of each item to the common component. These range from .716 to .837, so each item contributes sufficient to the component. The component explains 63% of the variance in the seven items, which is high. Cronbach's alpha (α) was calculated to establish the reliability of the scale. An alpha of .90 indicates that items form a very good scale.

For each respondent a score on privacy risk perception was calculated by adding the values on the seven items and dividing the sum by seven. Scores on privacy risk perception thus range from 1 (very low privacy risk perception) to 5 (very high privacy risk perception). The mean of privacy risk perception is 3.06 (see table 1), which is just above the scale mean of 3.00, meaning that on average, the respondents are neutrally concerned about privacy threats.

4.2   The use of privacy protection strategies

The strategies of reducing privacy threats were measured by 13 items in three groups. The first group, the behavioural measures consisted of three items: anonymous email addresses, pseudonyms and providing false information. The use of anonymous email address, was measured by asking: 'How many of these email addresses are anonymous email addresses?'. The figures provided were recoded into 'does not have an anonymous email address' and 'does have an anonymous email address'. The use of pseudonyms and providing incorrect answers were both measured on a five-point scale using the questions: 'Have you ever used a pseudonym, such as another name, alias, or nickname, in online activities when you were asked for your name?' and 'Have you ever intentionally given incorrect answers when you were asked for your personal information?'. The answers 'sometimes', 'frequently', and 'often' were, recoded into 'does use pseudonyms' respectively 'does provide incorrect answers. The answers 'never' and 'rarely' were recoded into 'does not use pseudonyms' and 'does not provide incorrect answers', respectively.

The remaining ten items, measuring the different strategies, were questions about the use of and familiarity with well known ('spam filters', 'firewalls', anti spyware) and lesser known ('encryption tools', 'anonymous remailers', 'trust certificates', 'anonymisers', 'cookie crunchers', 'password managers/vaults', and 'safe email') privacy enhancing technologies. The question was: 'How familiar are you with the following privacy enhancing technologies?'. The possible answers were: 'I use it', 'I'm familiar with it, but I don't use it', and 'I'm not familiar with it'.

Anonymous email addresses are used by 2760 respondents, which amounts for 55.8% of the sample population (see table 2). Within this group 54.5% is male against 45.5% female. The Chi square test (χ^2) reveals that this difference is real. On the basis of a 52% male sample, the expected proportion male anonymous email users is 2760 * 0.52 = 1435, whereas the actual proportion is 2760 * 0.545 = 1504. The same holds for the percentage men in the group who do not use anonymous email addresses, this percentage, 48.6%, is also different from the expected percentage.

Table 2. Use of strategies and gender and mean age in the different groups.

Strategy	Uses it	Does not use it
Anonymous email	2760 (55.8%)	2184 (44.2%)
Males (χ^2 (df=1) = 16.84***)	54.5%	48.6%
Age (t (df=3800) = 7.60***)	23.4	25.1
Pseudonyms	3189 (62.8%)	1885 (37.2%)
Males (χ^2 (df=1) = 240.44***)	60.4%	37.9%
Age (t (df=2937) = 7.77***)	23.5	25.3
Incorrect answers	2157 (45.3%)	2603 (54.7%)
Males (χ^2 (df=1) = 250.98***)	64.2%	41.1%
Age (t (df=4643) = 6.04***)	23.5	24.8

Note:* $p < .05$; ** $p < .01$; *** $p < .001$

The χ^2-test is significant at the $p < .001$ level, which means that the probability that the difference between the observed and expected frequencies exists due to chance is less than 0.1 percent. So, we may conclude that more men than women use anonymous email addresses and that there are more women than men in the group who do not use anonymous email addresses. The mean age in the group of those who use anonymous email addresses is 23.4 and the mean age of non users is 25.1. A t-test shows that these means differ significantly from each other. So, anonymous email addresses are more often used by younger people.

Pseudonyms are more often used than anonymous email addresses, 62.8% against 55.8%,, and they are more often used by men than women, 60.4% against 39.6%. The differences between men and women in the groups of pseudonym users and non pseudonym users again show a significant difference. Most people provide correct instead of incorrect answers when personal information is asked for, 54.7% against 45.3%, but incorrect answers are more often given by men than women (64.2% against 35.8%). Pseudonyms and incorrect answers are also more often used by younger people, 23.5 and 23.5 against 25.3 and 24.8, respectively.

With respect to the common privacy and security safeguards, it turns out that most respondents use spam filters, firewalls, and anti spyware, 79.0%, 88.5%, and 73.6% respectively (see table 3). Only a small number of people are unfamiliar with these Privacy Enhancing Technologies (ranging from 1.9% for firewalls to 7.9% for anti spyware). More men than women use these technologies, and also more men than women are familiar with spam filters and firewalls (but don't use them). In the groups of those who are unfamiliar with spam filters, firewalls, and anti spyware we see significantly more women than men, 75.7%, 77.9%, and 82.7% respectively. There is a small, but significant, difference between the mean age of those who use spam filters and firewalls and those who are familiar with these technologies. In contrast to using anonymous email addresses and pseudonyms and providing incorrect answers, spam filters and firewalls are more often used by older people, 24.7 and 24.5 against 23.4 and 23.4.

Encryption tools, anonymous remailers, trust certificates, cookie crunchers, password managers and vaults, and safe email are largely unknown to the respondents, percentages range from 42.1% to 69.7%, especially amongst women.

These technologies are more often used by men than women. Of the non-users men are, more often than women, more familiar with these technologies. An exception, however, is the use of password managers or vaults. These are more often used by women than by men. The largest difference between men and women can be seen in the use of encryption tools. No less than 85.3% of the people who use encryption tools are men. The people who use encryption tools or a familiar with them are significantly older than the people who are unfamiliar with this technology, 25.2 and 25.6 against 23.4. No differences in the average age were found between the users of anonymous remailers, anonymisers, cookie crunchers, password managers or vaults, and safe email, and those who are familiar (but don't use them) or are unfamiliar with these technologies.

Table 3. Use of and familiarity with strategies by gender.

Strategy	Uses it	Is familiar with it	Is unfamiliar with it
Spam filters	3169 (79.0%)	738 (18.4%)	103 (2.6%)
Males (χ^2 (df=2) = 41.72***)	53.5%	58.1%	24.3%
Age (F (df=2;4003) = 7.62***) 24.7		23.4	24.0
Firewalls	3538 (88.5%)	388 (9.7%)	74 (1.9%)
Males (χ^2 (df=2) = 30.49***)	54.6%	50.8%	23.0%
Age (F (df=2;3993) = 4.57*)	24.5	23.4	23.0
Anti spyware	2932 (73.6%)	740 (18.6%)	313 (7.9%)
Males (χ^2 (df=2) = 198.68***)	58.4%	49.6%	17.3%
Age (F (df=2;3978) = 1.99)	24.4	24.0	25.0
Encryption tools	667 (16.9%)	118 (30.1%)	2097 (53.1%)
Males (χ^2 (df=2) = 852.62***)	85.3%	73.8%	32.2%
Age (F (df=2;3945) = 34.29***)		25.2	25.6 23.4
Anonymous remailers	124 (3.1%)	1166 (29.4%)	2677 (67.5%)
Males (χ^2 (df=2) = 404.68***)	74.2%	76.8%	42.6%
Age (F (df=2;3960) = 4.13)	24.9	24.9	24.1
Trust certificates	1246 (31.3%)	1037 (26.1%)	1697 (42.6%)
Males (χ^2 (df=2) = 610.85***)	74.0%	65.5%	31.3%
Age (F (df=2;3973) = 2.84)	24.8	24.5	24.1
Anonymisers	113 (2.8%)	1095 (27.5%)	2774 (69.7%)
Males (χ^2 (df=2) = 431.53***)	75.2%	78.7%	42.7%
Age (F (df=2;3975) = 3.71)	23.4	24.9	24.2
Cookie crunchers	643 (16.1%)	1231 (30.9%)	2108 (52.9%)
Males (χ^2 (df=2) = 148.64***)	56%	67%	45.3%
Age (F (df=2;3975) = 0.23)	24.5	24.3	24.4
Password managers/vaults	836 (21.1%)	1461 (36.8)	1673 (42.1%)
Males (χ^2 (df=2) = 308.95***)	47.2%	71.6%	41.1%
Age (F (df=2;3963) = 0.31)	24.2	24.5	24.4
Safe email	380 (9.6%)	1298 (32.8%)	2285 (57.7%)
Males (χ^2 (df=2) = 222.87***)	59.2%	69.3%	43.7%
Age (F (df=2;3956) = 2.01)	23.6	24.5	24.5

Notes: * p < .05; ** p < .01; *** p < .001

The percentage of people who use behavioral privacy protection strategies or common PETs ranges from 45.3% for providing incorrect answers to 88.5% for firewalls. In contrast, the percentage of people who use advanced PETs ranges from 2.8% for anonymisers to 31.3% for trust certificates. So, hypothesis 1 is confirmed: behavioral privacy protection strategies and common PETs are more often used than advanced PETs.

To check for correlations between pairs of strategies, we used Phi when both strategies had only two answering options (i.e. use or don't use) and Cramer's V when at least one of the strategies had three answering options (i.e. use, familiar, or unfamiliar). The resulting correlation coefficient ranges from 0, no correlation, to -1 or +1, perfect correlation. Table 4 shows the correlation matrix. The three (theoretical) groups outlined previously (behavioral, common measures, more complex PETs) can clearly be distinguished here. The first group consists of using anonymous email addresses and pseudonyms, and providing incorrect answers. Low, positive, and significant correlations were found between these three strategies, ranging from .206 to .355. This indicates that using one of these strategies is slightly enhancing the possibility of the respondent also using the other two strategies as well. The use of anonymous email addresses and pseudonyms, and providing incorrect answers, however, is independent from the use of the more complex PETs, that is, using anonymous email addresses and pseudonyms, and providing incorrect answers do not influence the use of these more complex PETs, or vice versa.

The second group consists of spam filters, firewalls, and anti spyware. Here too, low, positive, and significant correlations between the strategies are found, ranging from .207 to .307. This indicates that using one of these technologies slightly increases the probability of using one of the other two technologies.

The third group consists of the technologies most people are unfamiliar with (i.e. encryption tools, anonymous remailers, trust certificates, anonymisers, cookie crunchers, password managers or vaults, and safe email). Between these technologies, low to moderate, positive and significant correlations were found, indicating that people who are unfamiliar with one of these technologies, are also likely to be unfamiliar with one of the other technologies.

We can, therefore, not clearly accept, nor reject hypothesis 4. There are positive relationships between strategies, but only between strategies within the same group (i.e. behavioral strategies, widely used PETs, and more advanced PETs).

4.3   Does privacy risk perception explain privacy protection strategy

An interesting research question is whether privacy risk perception explains the use of certain privacy protection strategies. On the basis of the current analysis this question can not be answered, we have no insight in the causality or finality of the relations. What we can do is see whether the privacy risk perception of users versus non-users (and within this latter group between those familiar with the technology and those not) of particular strategies differs. For this purpose we have used F-tests. If the F-test is significant, at least two group means are different from each other meaning that the perceptions in the various groups really differ. When the F-test was significant, a

Tukey HSD multiple comparisons Post Hoc test was used to determine which group means differ significantly from each other.

For the spam filters, firewalls, and anti spyware, the F-tests are not significant, which means that the privacy risk perception of the group who uses them is not different from the group who is familiar with them (but not uses them). And the privacy risk perception of those who are unfamiliar with these technologies is not different from those who use or are familiar with them (see table 5). So, hypothesis 2 is rejected for spam filters, firewalls, and anti spyware.

For encryption tools, the F-test is significant and the Tukey test shows that the mean privacy risk perception in the group who uses encryption tools is significantly different from the mean privacy risk perception in the group who is unfamiliar with this technology, 3.12 against 3.01. So, people who use encryption tools, on average, have a stronger privacy risk perception than those who are unfamiliar with encryption tools. The mean privacy risk perception of those who are familiar, but don't use, encryption tools is neither different from those who use this technology, nor from those who are unfamiliar with it. The same holds for trust certificates and password managers or vaults. The privacy risk perception of those who use these technologies is significantly stronger than the privacy perception of those who are unfamiliar with them.

For anonymous remailers, a significant difference in mean privacy risk perception was not only found between those who use them and those who are unfamiliar with them, but also between those who are familiar with them and those who are unfamiliar with them, but not between those who use them and those who are familiar with (but not use) them. Apparently, the privacy risk perception of those who are familiar with anonymous remailers, independent of whether one uses this technology or not, is stronger than the privacy risk perception of those who are unfamiliar with anonymous remailers. The same holds for anonymisers. Independent of whether the technology is used or not, those who are familiar with anonymisers have, on average, a stronger privacy risk perception than those who are unfamiliar with them.

Both for cookie crunchers and safe email, the F-test was significant and the Tukey test shows that, on average, the privacy risk perception of people who use these technologies is stronger than the privacy risk perception of people who do not use these technologies, irrespective whether one is familiar with the technology or not.

The F-test tests only whether the groups differ, but does not show how big the difference is, that is, what the effect size is. The effect size can be calculated, but only for two groups. Because there is no difference in privacy risk perception between those who are familiar with cookie crunchers and those who are not, but both groups differ from the group who use them, we have merged these groups to form a new group: 'does not use cookie crunchers'. The same was done for safe email resulting in the new group: 'does not use safe email'. For both anonymous remailers and anonymisers, the group who uses these technologies and the group who is only familiar with these technologies were merged.

Table 4. Correlations between privacy protection strategies

	anon. email	pseudon.	incorr. answ.	spam filters	Firewall	anti spywar.	encrypt.	anonyn. remailers	trust certs.	anony. miser	cookie crunch	pass. man/vlt
Pseudonyms	.253***a											
Incorrect answers	.206***a	.355***a										
Spam filters	.020b	.045*b	.061*b									
Firewalls	.018b	.063***b	.072***b	.307***b								
Anti spyware	.073***b	.157***b	.108***b	.207***b	.266***b							
Encryption	.078***b	.183***b	.188***b	.117***b	.095***b	.188***b						
Anonymous remailers	.097***b	.160***b	.165***b	.071***b	.104***b	.131***b	.387***b					
Trust certificates	.124***b	.241***b	.200***b	.123***b	.103****b	.188***b	.387***b	.325***b				
Anonymisers	.125***b	.187***b	.180***b	.063***b	.053***b	.120***b	.374***b	.613***b	.361***b			
Cookie crunchers	.076***b	.127***b	.103***b	.102***b	.063***b	.136***b	.256***b	.321***b	.235***b	.366***		
Password manager/vault	.089***b	.141***b	.133***b	.079***b	.061***b	.123***b	.294***b	.300***b	.267***b	.315***	.295***	
Safe email	.087***b	.139***b	.105***b	.068***b	.042***b	.100***b	.266***b	.330***b	.235***b	.361***	.323***	.380***

Notes: * $p < .05$; ** $p < .01$; *** $p < .001$
[a] value is Phi
[b] value is Cramer's V

Table 5. Differences in privacy risk perception in PET's strategy groups.

	Mean (SD)	F (df)	group means that differ significantly from each other[a]
Spam filters			
Uses it (1)	3.06 (.922)		
Is familiar with it (2)	3.00 (.943)		
Is unfamiliar with it (3)	3.08 (1.056)	F(2;3892) = 1.41	no differences
Firewalls			
Uses it (1)	3.06 (.928)		
Is familiar with it (2)	2.98 (.942)		
Is unfamiliar with it (3)	3.05 (.958)	F(2;3881) = 1.07	no differences
Anti spyware			
Uses it (1)	3.07 (.925)		
Is familiar with it (2)	3.02 (.928)		
Is unfamiliar with it (3)	2.96 (.977)	F(2;3869) = 2.31	no differences
Encryption			
Uses is (1)	3.12 (.914)		
Is familiar with it (2)	3.08 (.926)		
Is unfamiliar with it (3)	3.01 (.939)	F(2;3836) = 3.77*	1 and 3
Anonymous remailers			
Uses it (1)	3.28 (1.029)		
Is familiar with it (2)	3.13 (.919)		
Is unfamiliar with it (3)	3.00 (.927)	F(2;3852) = 11.59***	1 and 2, 2 and 3
Trust certificates			
Uses it (1)	3.09 (.904)		
Is familiar with it (2)	3.07 (.939)		
Is unfamiliar with it (3)	3.00 (.939)	F(2;3868) = 3.74*	1 and 3
Anonymisers			
Uses it (1)	3.30 (.977)		
Is familiar with it (2)	3.12 (.915)		
Is unfamiliar with it (3)	3.01 (.931)	F(2;3867) = 9.28***	1 and 3, 2 and 3
Cookie crunchers			
Uses it (1)	3.23 (.924)		
Is familiar with it (2)	3.06 (.917)		
Is unfamiliar with it (3)	3.00 (.934)	F(2;3867) = 15.09***	1 and 2, 1 and 3
Password manager/vault			
Uses it (1)	3.12 (.954)		
Is familiar with it (2)	3.07 (.921)		
Is unfamiliar with it (3)	3.00 (.925)	F(2;3854) = 4.46*	1 and 3
Safe email			
Uses it (1)	3.21 (.949)		
Is familiar with it (2)	3.07 (.916)		
Is unfamiliar with it (3)	3.06 (.931)	F(2;3850) = 7.13**	1 and 2, 1 and 3

Notes: * p < .05; ** p < .01; *** p < .001
[a] Tukey HSD multiple comparisons Post Hoc test was used

A series of t-tests were conducted to establish whether there was a difference in privacy risk perception between the two groups thus constructed for each PET. First the means on privacy risk perception of men were compared with that of women (see table 6). The t-test is not significant, indicating that men and women do not differ in their privacy risk perception. The (Pearson product-moment) correlation coefficient was calculated between age and privacy risk perception, showing that privacy risk perception is independent from age ($r = .013$, non significant; not reported in a table).

Table 6. Differences in privacy risk perception between men and women and in strategy groups.

	Mean (SD)	t(df) independent observations	Cohen's d
Men	3.05 (.914)		
Women	3.06 (.953)	t(4422) = -0.47	no difference
Anonymous email			
Uses it	3.13 (.912)		
Does not use it	2.95 (.948)	t(4069) = -6.40***	0.19
Pseudonyms			
Uses it	3.15 (.923)		
Does not use it	2.88 (.920)	t(3289) = -9.56***	0.29
Incorrect answers			
Uses it	3.15 (.890)		
Does not use it	2.97 (.958)	t(4230) = -6.45***	0.19
Encryption			
Uses it	3.11 (.914)		
Is unfamiliar with it	3.01 (.939)	t(1095) = 2.50*	0.11
Trust certificates			
Uses it	3.09 (.904)		
Is unfamiliar with it	3.00 (.939)	t(2662) = 2.59*	0.10
Password manager/vault			
Uses it	3.12 (.954)		
Is unfamiliar with it	3.00 (.925)	t(1566) = 2.83**	0.13
Anonymous remailers			
Uses it/is familiar with it	3.15 (.930)		
Is unfamiliar with it	3.00 (.927)	t(2466) = 4.51***	0.16
Anonymisers			
Uses it/is familiar with it	3.14 (.921)		
Is unfamiliar with it	3.01 (.931)	t(2263) = 3.90***	0.14
Cookie crunchers			
Uses it	3.23 (.924)		
Does not use it	3.02 (.928)	t(881) = 5.19***	0.23
Safe email			
Uses it	3.21 (.949)		
Does not use it	3.03 (.926)	t(439) = 3.35***	0.19

Note: * $p < .05$; ** $p < .01$; *** $p < .001$

Next, the privacy risk perception of the group 'anonymous email address users' was compared with that of the non-users. The t-test is significant and comparing the means leads to the conclusion that those who use anonymous email addresses, on average, have a stronger privacy risk perception than the non-users, 3.13 against 2.95. Cohen's d^4 was calculated to establish the effect size. Effect sizes with absolute values between 0.20 and 0.50 refer to small differences, between 0.50 and 0.80 to moderate ones, and above .80 to large ones [3]. The effect size for anonymous email is .19, so there is a small difference in privacy risk perception between those who use anonymous email addresses and those who don't. The difference in privacy risk perception between those who provide incorrect answers and those who don't is also significant, but again this is only a small difference. So, The groups who use anonymous email addresses and provide incorrect answers both have, on average, a stronger privacy risk perception than the groups who don't use anonymous email addresses and don't provide incorrect answers. The privacy risk perception of those who use pseudonyms is stronger than that of those who don't use pseudonyms, 3.15 against 2.88, but with a Cohen's d of .29 this is still a small difference. Hypothesis 2 is accepted for anonymous email addresses, pseudonyms, and incorrect answers, but an adjustment was made to the statement. People who use anonymous email addresses, pseudonyms, and incorrect answers have a somewhat stronger privacy risk perception than the people who don't use these strategies.

The privacy risk perception of those who use encryption tools, trust certificates, or password managers is significantly stronger than those who don't use these technologies, but these differences are very small. Also the effect sizes for anonymous remailers and anonymisers are very small, which is also apparent when looking at the means in privacy risk perception of those who are familiar with these technologies and those who are unfamiliar with them, 3,15 and 3.14 against 3.00 and 3.01. Hypothesis 2 is rejected for encryption tools, trust certificates, password managers or vaults, anonymous remailers, and anonymisers. The effect sizes for cookie crunchers and safe email are somewhat larger, but they are still small. So, The privacy risk perception of those who use cookie crunchers or safe email is, on average, stronger than that of those who don't use these technologies, 3.23 and 3.21 against 3.02 and 3.03. Hypothesis 2 is accepted for cookie crunchers and safe email, but an adjustment was made to the statement. People who use cookie crunchers and safe email have a somewhat stronger privacy risk perception than the people who don't use these strategies.

To establish whether the privacy risk perception of people who use advanced PETs is stronger than that of people who only use behavioral strategies or common PETs, the mean privacy risk perception of the both groups were compared. The t-test (t (df=4276) = -2.66**) shows that the mean privacy risk perception of people who use advanced PETs (3.10) is significantly different from that of people who only use behavioral strategies or common PETs (3.02), but Cohen's d indicates that this difference is extremely small and therefore negligible (Cohen's d = 0.08). So, we can therefore conclude that there is no difference with respect to privacy risk perception

---

[4] Cohen's d for independent observations.

between those who use advanced PETs and those who only use behavioral strategies or common PETs and hypothesis 3 is therefore rejected.

5   Discussion and conclusion

The analysis shows that privacy risk perception can be measured by the seven specific privacy threats. The correlation between the concerns about the individual privacy risks were high and the seven items form a good scale. This means that the questions employed can be used as an indicator for online privacy concern. When applied to our sample, the students in our sample appear to show only moderate (3.06 on a scale from 1 to 5) privacy concern.

With respect to the privacy protection strategies, unsurprisingly, spam filters, firewalls, and anti spyware are PETs that are used by almost everyone. Of course, these PETs have become standard tools on almost every computer and internet subscription plan, which means that people have easy access to them. The other strategies, behavioral measures and more complex PETs show a different picture. Behavioral measures: using anonymous email addresses, using pseudonyms, and providing false personal data, which although available to everyone, require more deliberation and decision making in their use. One has to make conscious decisions to use a pseudonym in an interaction or to lie about one's personal data. Furthermore, one has to realize that using these strategies is an option and that using this option may serve privacy protection. Judging from experiences we have gained in focus groups and classroom settings these insights are not completely common. Nevertheless, pseudonyms are used by about 63% of our sample, anonymous email addresses by 56% and providing false data by just 45%. Given the moderate privacy concerns of our sample, and the unclear merits of adopting these behavioral strategies these seem relatively large numbers. A partial explanation for the high numbers for pseudonyms and anonymous email addresses may be found in the fact that many students have Hotmail and Yahoo addresses that are also used to register for social network services such as MSN, Hyves, MySpace, Friendster, Flickr, and YouTube. Using made-up names is common in these services, and these networks are also used by their users to experiment with their identities which often implies the use of pseudonyms [4]. The third privacy protection strategy, the more advanced PETs are largely unknown to our respondents (Dutch students) and (consequently?) hardly employed. This is interesting given the responses to other questions in our survey that suggest that our respondents do feel a need for more computer programmes to protect their privacy, as well as tighter government regulation. How does this relate to our respondents' ignorance of existing applications?

All privacy protection strategies represented in our study are more often used by men than by women, with the exception of password managers or vaults, where women are the principal users. Why are women the principal users of password managers? Do they use more online identities which make identity management more complex calling for identity management solutions? Are they better organized? Men are also more often familiar with PETs than women. Does this reflect the fact that men generally are more interested in technology and do other kinds of things online? Why are women lagging behind? These are questions we will explore in future studies using our current survey data set as a starting point.

Looking more closely at the three groups of protection strategies, the first group, the widely used PETs, shows higher correlations with each other than with the other strategies, indicating that the use of either spam filters, firewalls, or anti spyware, reinforces the use of the other two. This may be due to the fact that spam filters and spyware protection are often provided by the user's internet provider. The group of behavioral strategies also shows higher correlations with each other than with the other strategies. So, using anonymous email addresses or pseudonyms or providing incorrect answers when personal information is requested, reinforces the use of the other two strategies. Here an explanation may be that once one has an anonymous email address, say BigHunk@yahoo.com, BigHunk most likely will also be used as a pseudonym in other interactions. This does, however, not explain the correlation with lying about one's personal data. Also the third group of strategies, the more advanced PETs, shows higher correlations amongst them than with the other strategies, indicating that using one more advanced PET reinforces the use of other more advanced PETs. Is the explanation here that many of the advanced PETs still have a 'geek' connotation?

Finally, our introductory question. Does a high privacy risk perception incur the use of privacy protecting measures? The present study does not answer this question directly. But the analysis does show some interesting findings. Firstly, respondents with high privacy risk perception are likely to be aware of measures they can take themselves. This means they are aware of the risks and the measures to lower these risks. Secondly, the privacy risk perception of users versus non-users of a particular protection strategy does not differ much for most strategies. And also there is no difference in privacy risk perception of those who use advanced PETs and those who only use behavioral strategies or common PETs. These two results suggest that a high privacy perception is an insufficient motivator for people to adopt privacy protecting strategies, while knowing these exist. The only (weak) exceptions to this conclusion are, (from highest to lowest difference in privacy risk perception between users and non-users) pseudonyms, cookie crunchers, anonymous email addresses, incorrect answers, and safe email. The people who use these measures have significantly higher privacy perceptions than those who don't use them. But in general, apparently, the use of privacy protection measures (strategies) is also dependent on other factors like access to the actual measures (such as a cookie cruncher). Another explanation may be that when people have a strong privacy risk perception they adopt protection measures which subsequently (or consequently) lowers their privacy risk perception. If high privacy concerns are not sufficient to motivate people, then what does?

Revising the initial model on the basis of the findings results in figure 2.

Some final remarks. We have presented the data for our sample as a whole and have only looked at age and gender differences. In our data the ethnicity of the respondents, the topic of their study and a detailed account of their online activities are recorded. In upcoming work we will analyze the data for different subgroups. From initial studies it is clear that privacy perceptions of various (ethnic) subgroups differs significantly. Whether this has an effect on their adoption of privacy protecting measures is an interesting question.

A second remark concerns our sample. We have surveyed a relatively large sample of university and colleges of higher education students in the Netherlands. The sample therefore is certainly not representative for the entire Dutch population, let alone for Europe. The privacy risk perception and the adoption of privacy protection strategies within a student population may significantly differ from the population as a whole. Students interact a lot with their peers and they behave in a similar way online. How does this compare to 30-40 year olds, or even 50-60 year olds? In our view people should be aware of the privacy risks they run in the online world. They also have to take measures within their reach to protect their own privacy. This desperately calls for a better understanding of what makes people adopt protection strategies.

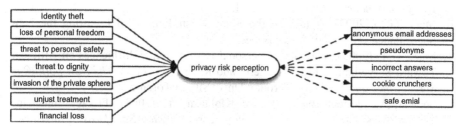

Fig. 2. Privacy risk perception and strategies (dotted lines reflect weak effects).

6 Acknowledgement

The work reported in this paper was supported by the IST PRIME project. The PRIME project receives research funding from the Community's 6th Framework Program (Contract No. 507591) and the Swiss Federal Office for Education and Science.

7 References

1. Buchanan, T., Paine, C., Joinson, A.N., & Reips, U. (2007). Development of Measures of Online Privacy Concern and Protection for Use on the Internet. *Journal of the American Society for Information Sciences and Technology, 58,* 157-165.
2. Burgoon, J.K., Parrott, R., LePoire, B.A., Kelley, D.L., Walther, J.B., & Perry, D. (2007). Maintaining and restoring privacy through communication in different types of relationships. *Journal of Social and Personal Relationships, 6,* 131-158.
3. Cohen, J. (1988). *Statistical power analysis for the behavioural sciences* (2nd ed.). Hillsdale, NJ: Erlbaum.

4. Donath, J. & boyd, d. (2004), Public display of connection, *BT Technology Journal, Vol 22, 4,* 71-82.
5. Hinkle, D.E., Wiersma, W., & Jurs, S.G. (1998). *Applied statistics for the behavioural sciences* (4th ed). Houghton Mifflin Company: Boston.
6. Introna, L.D. & Pouloudi, A. (1999). Privacy in the Information Age: Stakeholders, Interests and Values. *Journal of Business Ethics, 22,* 27-38.
7. Pallant, J. (2001). *SPSS Survival Manual. A step by step guide to data analysis using SPSS for Windows (Versions 10 and 11).* Open University Press: Buckingham.
8. Lyon, D. (2004). Globalizing Surveillance. Comparative and Sociological Perspectives *International Sociology, 19,* 135-149.
9. Marx, G.T. (1994). New Telecommunications Technologies And Emergent Norms. In G. Platt and C. Gordon (Eds.). *Self, Collective Behavior and Society. Essays in honour of Ralph Turner.* JAI.
10. Marx, G.T. (2003). A tack in the Shoe: Neutralizing and Resisting the New Surveillance. *Journal of Social Issues, 59,* 369-390.
11. Marx, G.T. (2006). Varieties of personal Information as Influences on Attitudes Toward Surveillance. In K. Haggerty and R. Ericson (Eds.). *The New politics of Surveillance and Visibility.* Toronto: University of Toronto Press.
12. Seničar, V., Jerman-Blažič, B., & Klobučar, T. (2003). Privacy-Enhancing Technologies – approaches and development. *Computer Standards & Interfaces, 25,* 147-158.
13. Solove, D.J. (2003). Identity Theft, Privacy, and the Architecture of Vulnerability. *Hastings Law Journal, 54,* 1227.
14. Stalder, F. (2002). The Failure of Privacy Enhacing Technologies (PETs) and the Voiding of Privacy. *Sociological Research Online, vol. 7, no. 2.* Accessible at http://www. socresonline.org.uk/7/2/stalder.html.
15. Westin, A. (1967). *Privacy and freedom.* New York: Atheneum.

8   Internet sources

http://www.epic.org/privacy/survey

A Contextual Method for Evaluating Privacy Preferences

Caroline Sheedy[1] and Ponnurangam Kumaraguru[2]

[1] Dublin City University
Glasnevin, Dublin 9, Dublin, Ireland
csheedy@computing.dcu.ie
[2] School of Computer Science
Carnegie Mellon University,
Pittsburgh, PA 15213
ponguru@cs.cmu.edu

Abstract. Identity management is a relevant issue at a national and international level. Any approach to identity management is incomplete unless privacy is also a consideration. Existing research on evaluating an individual's privacy preferences has shown discrepancies in the stated standards required by users, and the corresponding observed behaviour. We take a contextual approach to surveying privacy, using the framework proposed by contextual integrity, with the aim of further understanding users self reported views on privacy at a national level.

1 Introduction

Privacy is an inherent concern for users in electronic transactions. Such concerns are based in the lack of anonymity afforded by electronic transactions. Some personal data is usually required for completion of these transactions, such as name, address, preferences. Identity management systems aim to manage various partial identities, whereas a privacy-enhanced identity management system should prevent linkability between the partial identities of a user [10]. Brands argues that "Schemes in which users do not have control over their own personal data offer zero privacy " [2] . Privacy should be a design consideration of identity management schemes, not an add-on to a finished product. Privacy is pertinent to a wide range of arenas: social, legal, technical etc.

Forming an understanding about privacy perceptions and concerns of individuals is generally achieved by conducting privacy surveys [6, 8]. The most prolific privacy surveyor is Dr. Alan Westin [7].

1.1 Motivation

By analysing a privacy survey using a contextual method, we hope to garner further insight into users privacy attitudes. As privacy is increasingly considered at a national and international level, it is necessary to have a consistent and effective means of comparing surveys.

Please use the following format when citing this chapter:

Sheedy, C. and Kumaraguru, P., 2008, in IFIP International Federation for Information Processing, Volume 261; *Policies and Research in Identity Management*; Eds. E. de Leeuw, Fischer-Hübner, S., Tseng, J., Borking, J.; (Boston: Springer), pp. 139–146.

1.2 Privacy Surveys

Privacy surveys are conducted to with a view to identifying people's conception of privacy, and their attitudes on how their personal information is collected and used [4]. They suffer from the 'talk is cheap' problem [3]. That is, users may state any preferences they like, without due consideration of the consequences.

Existing privacy survey methods have some associated issues [3, 11]. One such consideration is the survey design as it can skew results and manipulate responses. Another is finding a correlation between what respondents say and what they actually do [3]. The lack of comparability of independent studies is yet another issue. The factors affecting this include context, wording and sample size.

A valid question is "What should privacy surveys results be used for?". Surveys may be used as a means to evaluate public opinion, rather than dictate policy. As the need for international concurrence in this area increases, so too does the requirement for a means to effectively evaluate findings of such surveys.

2 Background

2.1 Contextual Integrity

Contextual integrity (CI) [9] was developed as an alternate benchmark for evaluating privacy breaches, in response to greater challenges from emerging technologies. Two of the fundamental concepts underlying CI are *contexts* and *norms*.

Contexts model societal structure, reflecting the core concept that society has distinctive settings. For example, society distinguishes between the social contexts of a hospital and a university. CI allows individuals to describe their privacy expectations, by associating norms of behaviour with contexts. The notion of a context and its norms mirror societal structure. In contrast to other privacy theories, CI associates the context with the subject's attribute being passed. Whether or not the data in question is confidential is often not the issue - information may only be deemed sensitive with respect to certain contexts.

CI uses norms of transmission to describe the accepted ways in which information may be passed. This reflects the accepted data flows within a context. These norms are used to describe a context, and they facilitate the sharing of data in a prescribed manner. Data gathering and dissemination must be appropriate to the stated norms of a context. For example, a student may accept their examination results being known within their academic department, as this is a norm within a university. They may not accept their results being passed outside of the university, as this would change the context in which the data flows.

Originating in a social and legal setting, CI postulates that *there are no arenas of life not governed by norms of information* [9]. It aims to provide users with an intuitive way to state their preferences. For instance, students naturally describe the limited sets of people that should access their examination results. They reference the context (university), the agents involved (employees, other students), their associated roles (finance, teaching), and the actual data (fees, results) to be passed. This facilitates the prescription of acceptable data flows as well as describing existing ones.

There are two types of norms: *norms of appropriateness* and *norms of distribution*. *Norms of appropriateness* address what information it is pertinent to disclose about a subject in a given context. For example, it is relevant for academic affairs to know details of a student's fee status to facilitate registration. Equally relevant, however, is to know what is not appropriate, such as details of a student's fee status being passed on to another student. This highlights the importance of relationships in norms. *Norms of distribution*, or flow, address the movement of information from one party to another. A finance office employee typically may only pass the students fee details to an employee of academic affairs. Thus, in order to ensure norms are respected, both the appropriateness and the distribution are considered.

2.2 Relevance of Context

Hine and Eve [4] observe that no single type of information is considered personal in all situations. Described as 'situated privacy', users associate a context with their privacy choices. Notions of privacy are found to be socially constructed, and CI was introduced as a means to mirror socially accepted norms of privacy. Combining these concepts, we analyse a survey on privacy preferences using a CI structure. This allows us to examine the complex nuances of privacy with a novel approach.

One suggestion [1] is to allow users to view their information in different circumstances. For example, the information they would be prepared to give to a retailer may differ from that which they would give to a marketer. CI offers a means to do this, by showing the associated contexts and norms of flow for a specific piece of information.

The need for context as a consideration of privacy surveys has been identified [6]. People will reveal data which they consider to be the 'norm', or typical for the given group or context. By discovering such norms using CI, survey results could aid in the design of an identity management system. Respondents were also found to only reveal atypical data which paints them in a positive light - people who has a slightly below average weight were happy to publicise this. Context is once again emphasised as an important factor of privacy.

2.3 Sample Survey

A study of international attitude differences with respect to privacy between the USA and India is carried out in [8]. They use the method of "mental models", with one-on-one interviews with 57 subjects. They drew interesting results on the differences in the national privacy perceptions of the subjects from the United State and those from India. We re-evaluate the responses from the Indian participants using a contextual approach. We aim to derive accepted norms of flow from the responses.

2.4 Culture

Hofstede [5] identifies two types of cultures, *collectivism* and *individualism*, and discusses the divide between them. A collectivist society uses 'we' as a major source of identity, whereas individualist societies expects individuals to identify as 'I'. Hofstede

[5] develops a number of cultural indices which measure the differences between societies. Of particular relevance is the Individualism Index (IDV), which measures how collectivist or individualist a society is. As India has a low IDV score, it is considered a collectivist society. Collectivist societies consider harmony with one's social environment a key virtue. Group interests prevail over those of the individual. In contrast to this, the USA is the highest ranking individualist society in Hofstede's study. He details the difficulties associated with culturally biased approaches to studies, and evaluating them. The survey used [8] follows Hofstede's recommendation of involving researchers from different cultures when developing questions.

CI [9] was developed by western minds, used to a culture of individualism. We examine its applicability to a non-individualistic culture by applying it to the surveys of the Indian respondents [8].

3   Analysis

3.1   Survey Details

The 14 questions posed in the survey protocol [8] were examined. It was decided to re-evaluate questions 1-10 only, as they covered the main areas of interest. They include general understanding and concerns about privacy, awareness of and concerns about privacy and technology, concerns about identity theft and knowledge of and concerns about data collection in organisations and government. The responses were considered in terms of dichotomies such as sensitive or non-sensitive, public or private and safe or unsafe, with the aim of uncovering accepted norms of information flow.

The survey was conducted via one-on-one open-ended interviews with respondents from India and the USA. Unfortunately, the original transcripts are unavailable from the participants in the USA. We had access to the 29 transcripts from the Indian subjects. The population sampled is not to be considered as statistically representative of any particular community or of technology users [8], consisting largely of college educated people who are familiar with the Internet.

3.2   Template

Question 1 "When you hear the word privacy, what comes to mind?"
Respondents considered privacy as one of two things: physical privacy and informational privacy. Over half of the respondents focused solely on privacy as a physical issue. They cited the contexts of home and work. The remainder considered privacy in terms of personal information. The respondents cited the contexts of social life, political, economic and online. Two respondents considered privacy as both information and physical.

A general trend in the nature of privacy concerns in respondents who considered privacy to be physical space throughout the survey was noted. Their concerns were focused on more traditional contexts, for example people looking at their monitor in an office or looking at paper based bank statements and credit cards in a bank. Respondents who considered privacy in terms of personal information focused on privacy concerns caused by existing and emerging technologies, such as data being disseminated electronically without their permission.

Question 2 "Do you have any (other) concerns about privacy?"

Out of the 29 respondents, 14 stated they had no privacy concerns. The remainder stated they had privacy concerns, and gave examples containing a context and sensitive data. This highlights the data that is considered private or sensitive such as financial, email, religion, background. The associated contexts identified were personal sphere, professional sphere and family.

With almost half of the respondents stating they had no privacy concerns, some cultural insight is given by one respondent: *".. the Indian culture has a system which says we should not hide anything...everything is common"*. This is reflective of a collectivist society.

Question 3 "Keeping computerised information secure, and out of the hands of people and groups that should not have it, is a problem that overlaps the issue of privacy. Tell me any concerns you may have."

Responses here were consistent. All users, except one, felt that some control mechanism was required to house the data securely. Four respondents specifically mentioned control over information dissemination. The respondent who was unconcerned felt that increasing accessibility to all data was a positive thing.

Users are happy to store their data electronically as long as access control mechanisms are place. Context was not a feature of most responses. Many respondents felt that either their personal data was not of interest to others, again a feature of the group 'we' mentality of a low IDV culture.

Question 4 "Data security and privacy are not really a problem because I have nothing to hide."

The majority of respondents, 22, disagreed with this. The remaining 7 deemed it acceptable to have all data public.

The responses to this question included free choice, confidentiality and necessity as factors in information flow. These factors correlate to the prominent norms of flow of CI.

Question 5 "Do you feel that information about you is exclusively yours, and the people who you ask to take the information?"

24 respondents agreed with this statement, with 18 stating that an individual maintains control of the information is disseminated about them, and 6 stating that this should be true, but was unrealistic in many contexts, such as online. The remaining 5 did not agree, as they felt data should be public.

The majority of respondents who agreed with this statement focused the situation where the information is passed by the individual. There was no mention of their data being passed on by others. No respondents brought up contentious issues, such as the entitlement of a sexual partner to know of their partner's HIV status.

Question 6 "Are you concerned about authorities misusing personal data of yours or members of your family?"

The 12 respondents who expressed concern here focused on potential misuse of their data by individuals within an organisation, rather than a corporate misused of their data. The remaining 17 had no concerns.

This question highlights the difference between low and high IDV cultures. CI emphasises the right to control information about oneself. This is a facet of a a high IDV culture. The trust placed in authorities by the majority of respondents is reflective of the belief system of low IDV cultures. Should majority opinion be enforced by policy or law in this case, a free for all with regard to data mining, dissemination and collection would occur. This is an example of CI highlighting areas of concern.

Question 7 "Are you concerned about the government misusing personal data of yours, or members of your family?"
Just over half, 16, stated they are unconcerned. Reasons such as the government is restricted by laws and they can only garner statistical knowledge of the data were given. The remaining 13 stated they are concerned.

This supports the observations of question 6 above. Applying the government-private dichotomy of political and legal inquiry of CI to this question results in a stale mate, with almost equal number on either side. A core principle of privacy theory is to protect the privacy of individuals against intrusive governments [9]. This opens the question as to what to do at a international level in the case of cultures where such concerns are not the norm. CI has been designed from a high IDV point of view, and considers the desire for privacy protection from invasive governments an objective. Thus, it is valid to question if CI can be applied to low IDV cultures.

Question 8 "Do you feel that more information collected on you and others will increase domestic security? Does it make you feel safer?"
The majority of respondents, 22 felt safer with the data being collected. Of these, 8 required that the data collected should be used in the context of national security only. The remaining 7 felt it was invasive, and open to abuse should the data flow out of context.

The context of the data played a big part of the response. A norm could be derived stating that data collected for national security cannot be used for any other reason, and that it must be securely stored. This would appease the concerns of those in favour of it, as well as addressing those against it.

Question 9 "Are you concerned about identity theft?"
17 respondents had no concerns regarding identity theft, feeling that no one would want to do this to them. A cultural norm of reflecting this trust could be drawn. The 12 who claimed to be concerned said they counteracted it using protection such as control over dissemination of information and passwords.

The data associated with identity theft by the respondents was tangible - passwords, passports, credit cards. It was felt self protection was possible, with one respondent stating that they didn't believe such things to happen in India. Thus the norm stating no concerns, so long as protection measures such as passwords and firewalls are used is possible here.

Question 10 "Consider technologies that exist today, or that soon might be developed. Are there some that you think pose a threat to privacy or data security?"
17 respondents expressed concern regarding technology, citing phones, access control cards etc as examples. The rest were aware of issues, but overall felt that technology is improving privacy and advances were generally viewed in a positive light.

Existing technological concerns focused on mobile phones and cameras.

4   Discussion

The re-evaluation of the data using a contextual method further highlights the differences between the expectations of a high IDV culture and the choices of a low IDV one. CI is proposed as a framework for stating privacy concerns. However, our findings suggest that CI needs to be extended to incorporate a low IDV culture. CI expects users to be concerned about privacy invasiveness. A significant number of survey respondents do not consider privacy concerns in terms of their personal data. They either trust the government and authorities to do the correct thing, or they consider privacy in terms of personal space. So there is a need to think about the underlying model of CI to incorporate the low IDV culture expectations.

Further work is required to design a privacy survey which captures the attitudes of international respondents. We believe that context should be a factor, as well as how to pose questions which garner the views of high and low IDV societies alike.

Acknowledgements

The authors would like to thank Dr. Stephen Blott from Dublin City University and Dr. Lorrie Cranor, Dr. Raj Reddy, Dr. Granger Morgan, and Elaine Newton from Carnegie Mellon University.

References

1. M.S. Ackerman, L.F. Cranor, and J. Reagle. Privacy in e-commerce: examining user scenarios and privacy preferences. *Proceedings of the 1st ACM conference on Electronic commerce*, pages 1–8, 1999.
2. S.A. Brands. *Rethinking Public Key Infrastructures and Digital Certificates: Building in Privacy.* MIT Press, 2000.
3. J. Harper and S. Singleton. With a Grain of Salt: What Consumer Privacy Surveys Dont Tell Us. *Competitive Enterprise Institute, June,* 2001.
4. C. Hine. Privacy in the Marketplace. *The Information Society*, 14(4):253–262, 1998.
5. G.J. Hofstede. *Cultures and Organizations: software of the mind.* McGraw-Hill, 2005.
6. BA Huberman, E. Adar, and LR Fine. Valuating Privacy. *Security & Privacy Magazine, IEEE*, 3(5):22–25, 2005.
7. P. Kumaraguru and L.F. Cranor. Privacy Indexes: A Survey of Westins Studies. *Institute for Software Research International*, 2005.
8. P. Kumaraguru, L.F. Cranor, and E. Newton. Privacy Perceptions in India and the United States: An Interview Study. *The 33rd Research Conference on Communication, Information and Internet Policy (TPRC), Sep,* 30:26–30, 2005.

9. H. Nissenbaum. Privacy as Contextual Integrity. *Washington Law Review*, 79(1):119–157, 2004.

10. A. Pfitzmann and M. Hansen. Anonymity, Unlinkability, Unobservability, Pseudonymity, and Identity Management-A Consolidated Proposal for Terminology. *Version v0*, 27:20, 2006.

11. M. Teltzrow and A. Kobsa. Impacts of User Privacy Preferences on Personalized Systems: a Comparative Study. *Designing Personalized User Experiences for eCommerce*, 2004.

Authentication

Implementing Strong Authentication Interoperability with Legacy Systems

Jan Zibuschka and Heiko Roßnagel

Johann Wolfgang Goethe University Frankfurt,
Chair for Mobile Business and Multilateral Security, Gräfstraße 78,
60054 Frankfurt am Main, Germany,
zibuschka@m-lehrstuhl.de, mail@heiko-rossnagel.de

Abstract. In a WWW environment, users need to come up with passwords for a lot of different services, e.g. in the area of e-commerce. These authentication secrets need to be unrelated if the user does not want to make himself vulnerable to insider attacks. This leads to a large number of passwords that a user has to generate, memorize, and remember. This password management is quite straining for users. Single sign on systems provide a solution for this dilemma. However, existing solutions often require the implementation of specific interfaces by the individual service providers, and usually do not support existing strong authentication factors, e.g. smart cards, without protocol extensions or modification of implementations. In this paper we propose a different approach that generates strong passwords using electronic signatures. Our approach builds on existing smart card infrastructures to achieve strong authentication, while at the same time it provides an interface to legacy password authentication systems.

1 Introduction

In a modern web environment, users need to come up with passwords for a lot of different services. Examples are web based mail, e-commerce sites and discussion forums. Passwords are also widely used for authentication in email, operating system login, remote shells, databases and instant messaging. This leads to a large number of passwords that a user has to generate, memorize, and remember. However, remembering a lot of randomly selected, independent passwords is quite straining for users, especially if some passwords are used only occasionally. Users tend to either choose weak passwords [4], or choose related passwords for several or even all accounts [2], which makes the authentication system vulnerable to cross-service attacks [11].

Furthermore, forgotten passwords are a major problem and an economic factor. A recent study estimates that help desk staff has to reset user passwords manually in 82% of cases [14]. This procedure often takes more than 5 minutes. As forgotten passwords are a common usability problem, this may result in high help desk costs. Additionally, the distraction and the time spent on resetting the password will reduce the productivity of users [14].

Please use the following format when citing this chapter:

Zibuschka, J. and Roßnagel, H., 2008, in IFIP International Federation for Information Processing, Volume 261; *Policies and Research in Identity Management*; Eds. E. de Leeuw, Fischer-Hübner, S., Tseng, J., Borking, J.; (Boston: Springer), pp. 149–160.

There are several authentication systems that are generally expected to offer a stronger security than passwords, such as public key cryptography in conjuncture with tokens. However, market penetration and usage of such systems has not lived up to expectations, and they often require the implementation of specific interfaces by the individual service providers.

We present a solution that integrates one such infrastructure, namely signature-capable smart cards, with password-based authentication mechanisms, offering single sign on functionality to the user, without requiring the implementation of specific interfaces by service providers. Implementing such protocols obviously consumes some resources. Also, replacing passwords as an authentication mechanism may add complexity, and as of such entrance barriers, thus losing the service provider users. Additionally, it may not be in service provider's best interest to standardize in the area of authentication due to the underlying network effects, based on phenomena such as lock-in and network externalities [21]. Still, compatibility is a major issue with regard to the overall value of the network. As [6] points out, "links in networks are potentially complementary but it is compatibility that makes complementary actual".

This paper is structured as follows: In section 2 we analyze requirements such a system has to meet. Based on that knowledge, we present our implementation of our system in section 3. We then discuss the advantages and disadvantages of our approach in section 4 before we conclude our findings in section 5.

2   Requirements

Apart from storing passwords in an encrypted form, it is also possible to generate them on the fly, using strong cryptography. However, such methods have to meet several requirements to guarantee their usefulness for user and service provider.

Our system's main concern is building a secure, interoperable authentication infrastructure on legacy systems (smart card infrastructures and password authentication mechanisms), rather than e.g. aiding anonymous service usage [8]. Several requirements can be derived from this scenario, and will be listed in this section.

- **Consistency:** For each web site, each user should be transparently provided with a consistent password.
- **Security of Generated Passwords:** The service passwords must be pseudorandom and independent. Additionally, the system must not leak information about the central authentication secret (in this case, the private signature key). Furthermore, a service password for any site must not give any information on any other service password. As a corollary, generated passwords should be chosen from a suitably large set, and should be ideally equidistributed, to avoid efficient (e.g. dictionary) attacks focusing on a specific, more probable subset.
- **Single Secret:** Given a single secret, e.g. a secret signature key or master password, the system should generate secure, distinct passwords for each web site.

The central secret should be protected using the strongest available measures, as it is also a single point of failure [14]. Preferably, the usage of a single secret should not be enforced, but it should rather be an option for the user to employ several secrets, if he deems it necessary.

- **Compliance with Password Policies:** Each generated password needs to be accepted by the web site, e.g. it must comply with the service's password policy.
- **Interoperability:** The architecture should be able to build on existing smart card or public key infrastructures (PKIs). To make the system easily deployable on top of e.g. an existing signature card infrastructure, we would prefer to use only algorithms that are present on all smart cards that can produce digital signatures. Additionally, service passwords should not be stored on the smart card, as publicly accessible memory is not present on all cards, and generally is less widespread than signature-related smart card applications.
- **Pervasiveness:** We aim for inter-device mobility, making storage of authentication information on the device impractical. Additionally, the implemented authentication mechanism should be performable on mobile devices, in spite of their limited performance.
- **Minimal Insider Attacks:** Unlike protocols employing an authentication proxy, we aim to realize a protocol that cannot be executed by a third party alone, to thwart insider attacks. The same holds true for the individual service providers, who in the classic password scenario could leverage the tendency of users to reuse passwords at several services [14] for cross-service attacks [3].
- **Usability:** The system should require minimal user interaction, as each necessary interaction step significantly reduces the acceptance of security-related systems. It has been stated that "The user base for strong cryptography declines by half with every additional keystroke or mouse click required to make it work." ("Ellison's Law") [3].
- **Minimal Provider Costs:** We aim to minimize necessary server infrastructure, while still meeting the interoperability and usability requirements.

3   Implementation

We implemented a prototype of our proposed password generator in Java. This allows for easy porting of the core components and easy deployment on many platforms, including mobile devices and various host applications, for example web browsers. The implementation uses signatures for the generation of account specific passwords. For signature creation we used a SIM card that was developed during the WiTness project sponsored by the European Union. This was chosen as an arbitrary existing SIM card infrastructure, demonstrating the adaptability of our system. It offers strong cryptographic algorithms, namely it is capable of creating RSA signatures [15] and also provides 3DES encryption. Other features of the SIM, like the encryption capability, might also have been used. However, the focus of deployed cards seems to be on digital signature capabilities, so these were also used for the password creation process.

3.1   Overview

We implemented a pluggable architecture, designed to make adding new smart card APIs or other authentication factors easy. Also, password encoder and transmission components have been designed to be easy to replace (see Figure 1). An additional benefit of this modular approach is a small, portable core containing the key algorithms.

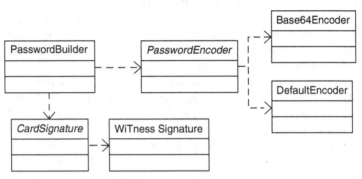

Fig. 1. Schematic Class Diagram

The basic data flow can be summarized in four steps [17]:

1. Define a scheme for deriving service identifiers for the different service providers the user might want to authenticate to. This can be implemented by concatenating several attributes of the service, such as a service name, URL, user's login name, IP address, and so on.
2. Combine the identifier for the service with the user's master password using strong cryptography [1] [8].
3. Transform the resulting value into a pseudorandom account password. This step is described in more detail in section 3.2.
4. Transfer the password to the appropriate service login form. This may be realized by an application that integrates with current browsers, maybe as a plug-in [9] [16]. Other implementations that generate passwords for additional services, such as database access or remote login are also possible.

Several cryptographic primitives, such as hash functions [1], signatures or a combination of algorithms [8], are suitable for step 2. As already mentioned, this paper focuses on signatures, for deployment reasons. Also, unkeyed hash functions have no secret that could be stored on the smart card.

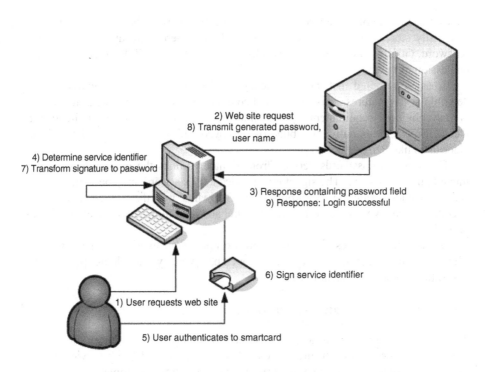

Fig. 2. Password Generation Using Smart Cards [17]

Like hash functions, electronic signatures can be used to generate strong service passwords for the user. Unlike hash functions, digital signatures have the security property of unforgeability, meaning that an attacker can't produce the user's signature for any text if he does not have the secret key, even if he is given the user's public key and several examples of signed messages. This would also translate to passwords. An attacker cannot compute any of the user's service passwords without knowing the secret key stored on the smartcard, even if he knows the user's passwords for several other accounts. The whole process is illustrated in Figure 2.

When the user needs to authenticate to an e-commerce site (1-3), the local system first derives the service identifier from the available context information, such as the accessed service's domain name and IP address (4). The user authenticates to the smart card using his PIN, thus unlocking the private signature key (5). The service identifier for the relevant account is then signed by the signature card using the private key, producing an electronic signature (6). The resulting value is encoded as a password (7). This is a critical step. While unforgeability is guaranteed due to the fact that signatures are used, the distribution and set size of generated passwords are also a factor for security of the system - it needs to output passwords chosen from a suitably large set, and may not employ an overly skewed selection algorithm. The transcoded signature is transmitted to the service provider requiring authentication, along with the user's login name (8). Access to the protected resources is then granted (9).

One advantage of this approach is that the central secret – the user's private key – is actually stored on the smart card and not directly dependent upon a user chosen password. Guessing the PIN will only allow access to this key if the attacker is also in possession of the token.

It has to be noted that the consistency requirement can only be achieved using deterministic signatures. This limits the theoretical strength of the system; however, it is an obvious requirement when interfacing with password authentication mechanisms. Additionally, the bulk of deployed infrastructures use deterministic algorithms like RSA or DSA.

The usage of passwords derived from signatures links the user's identity to his intent to use the service. The signature, encoded as a password, may be verified by the service provider using the user's public key. To realize this, the service provider first decodes the password to the original signature, and then follows the usual verification procedure.

Of course, signatures in this scenario are not linked to individual transactions. This is due to the fact that the widely deployed password systems do not perform user authentication on a transaction level.

3.2   Transcoding Signatures to Passwords

This can be done using e.g. a simple Base64 encoding, although more complicated schemes may be used to ensure the compliance of passwords with service policies [16]. In our solution, more complex transcoding algorithms are implemented to make up for restrictions of the used signature algorithms (e.g. signature distributions dependent on public keys, such as the RSA modulus) and requirements of service authentication mechanisms (e.g. password policies); to optimize compliance with password policies, output domain and statistic distribution of generated passwords.

As service passwords are generated pseudorandomly, the widely enforced password policies form an obstacle to this approach. They are usually not available in a format that would be machine readable by e.g. a SSO browser extension. The user may manually edit the produced passwords to suit the policy; however, this is error-prone and awkward.

Policy parameters might be input by the user for each service. However, to facilitate this approach, the number of parameters should be quite small, preferably with sensible defaults. Password length, distinction of upper-case and presence of numbers or special characters seem like a sensible set of parameters. To minimize user interaction, we will assume that policy information is supplied by a server, or a default policy suiting most services is employed. For a detailed overview of a policy input UI, see [7]. A complete overview of the set of parameters used in our system is given in Table 1.

While this set is not suitable to precisely describe all password policies in use, it is able to model an acceptable subset for each policy to the best knowledge of the authors, and a similar approach was successfully employed for [16]. In [9], another approach is proposed, but it cannot guarantee presence of certain character classes, and uses a significantly larger parameter set.

Table 1. Parameters for Password Policy Configuration

Password Policy Parameter	Legal Values
relevantUpperCase	true, false
hasNumberCharacter	true, false
hasSpecialCharacter	true, false
passwordLength	positive integer {...6, 7, 8, 9....}
specialCharactersUsed	String (set of special characters in use)

Note that the character sets marked as true are not only possible, but required for all generated service passwords. Having separate parameters for this is possible, but would lead to additional clutter of the user interface for inputting policies. Passwords generated in this way will still be stronger than user passwords, because of the length and pseudorandomness of generated service passwords.

To realize random password generation based on those parameters, the simple armoring step (using e.g. Base64) for transformation in the encoding step 3 will have to be replaced by a more sophisticated encoding scheme. We propose a 2 step process.

In a first step, the generated signature material is adjusted to be equidistributed in a range needed by the next stage, e.g. it has to be transformed from pseudorandomly chosen over the signature output domain, defined by e.g. the RSA modulus in the case of RSA, to pseudorandomly chosen from a set of legal passwords, or several pseudorandomly chosen characters. For this, a stream base conversion method similar to the one described in [19] is employed.

In the second step, the renormalized pseudorandom material output by the first step is then transformed to part of a password (e.g. a character), parameterized with the service provider's password policy. One representative for each used character subset is generated, and then the remainder of the password is filled with random characters from the entire used character domain. In pseudo-code, using parameter names from Table 1:

```
password = ''
password.append(random_lower_case_character())
if (relevantUpperCase)
   password.append(random_upper_case_character())
if (hasNumberCharacter)
   password.append(random_number_character())
if (hasSpecialCharacter)
   password.append(
     random_special_character(specialCharactersUsed)
   )
while (password.length<passwordlength)
   password.append(random_legal_character())
do_random_permutation(password)
```

The last operation, do_random_permutation, signifies a permutation of the password's characters. While this will widen the set of possible outputs (e.g. not all output passwords start with a lower case letter), it somewhat skews the equidistribution. While the algorithm by does not offer a perfect distribution of service passwords, and is also restricted to a subset of service passwords allowed under certain password policies. Still, it offers a notable improvement over typical user-chosen passwords, and reaches password length and randomness that is hard to match even by careful users. Equidistribution of created passwords can be reached by omitting the permutation step. However, this will further reduce the output password subset.

3.3   User Interface

The prototype user interface is quite straightforward, as shown in Figure 3. There are input fields for a service identifier (which may be e.g. the domain name of the service in the web surfing case) and the login the user chose for the service. Additional components, e.g. the service IP address, may also be used. The input may be provided by the user, or the fields may be filled automatically using data from the application used to contact the service (for example, by embedding it in a web browser plug-in [16]). In this case, the only things the user has to provide are the signature card and the PIN necessary to authenticate to it.

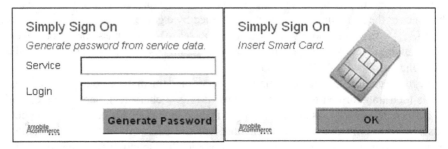

Fig. 3. Application screenshots

After the card is activated, an identification string for the relevant account is created by concatenating service identifier and user login. This string representation of the account is then signed using the existing signature mechanism. The account identifier is digitally signed in the usual fashion. The signature value is then transformed into a password string, as described in section 3.2.

The resulting password is copied to the system clipboard for transfer to an arbitrary host application.

We presume that a simple user interface such as described here will be best suited for meeting the simplicity requirement raised in section 2. However, enabling transparent (or, at least, minimally invasive) support for changing password policies on the server side will require additional effort. In [12], manually adjusting the generated password to meet the needs of the service is proposed. However, this will be straining for the user. For the time being, we just assume that a system similar to the service meta-information server described in [7] will be in place, and the formatting information be retrieved from there (or from a local cache, although that solution will hinder cross-system availability and thus pervasive applicability of the authentication solution).

4 Discussion

In contrast to conventional smart card solutions that store encrypted passwords on the token, our system can be deployed on top of already existing signature card infrastructure, thus limiting costs for the user and also the amount of authentication tokens the user has to manage.

Recently, governments across Europe have issued [5] [10] [20] or plan to issue signature capable identity cards as an e-government measure. For our prototype implementation we used a signature capable SIM card, demonstrating the viability of the algorithm in a mobile scenario. However, identity cards could also be used for the signature generation. Therefore, our solution could be implemented on top of e-government infrastructures already deployed in some European countries, such as the ones mentioned above. Furthermore, by using a SIM card for signature creation our solution could be implemented on a mobile phone, leveraging infrastructure provided by mobile operators [18]. It may be based either on already deployed SIM cards (if the algorithms present on the card allow for appropriate security guarantees), or rolled out together with signature-enabled SIMs to add a compelling use case.

The generated service passwords are directly dependent upon the user's cryptographic signature keys. If the user's key pair needs to be replaced, because e.g. it has been revoked, all the generated service passwords will change. While this poses a serious usability barrier in the described basic version of the system, saving account meta-information on a server can improve user experience during this and other use cases. The system is able to iterate over all the accounts, using the same architecture as the master password changing assistant in [7]. Note that, while the revoked key pair's signatures can no longer be verified, they may of course still be encoded and submitted as passwords.

Of course, in a SSO system, loss of the central secret – the secret key on the smart card token - means loss of all derived passwords. This paper does not discuss mechanisms for ensuring the robustness with regard to lost passwords in detail. However, most services offer a means to reset or retrieve a lost password. Additionally, conventional methods, like saving encrypted password lists to a secure storage as a backup, may be used.

As is pointed out in [1] [8], unlinkable user pseudonyms may also be generated in a similar fashion, which would be especially useful when combined with anonymous communication channels, based on e.g. TOR [8].

The card is portable but it is – in many cases, for example where signature cards are deployed as part of e-government initiatives - not obvious that it is used as a SSO token, so the security risks of portability are partially mitigated.

Also, the portability of the smart card token, along with the pervasiveness offered by the algorithm's operability without saved passwords, suggest implementing the system on mobile terminals. There are functions on standard-issue GSM SIMs that may take up the role of the signature algorithm presented in this paper. However, real-life implementations of these functions are dependent on the individual mobile operator. Also, keys are often shared between subscriber and mobile operator. So, while the system may be easily implementable if a signature-capable card is implemented in a mobile terminal, employing standard-issue SIMs for a similar functionality will require additional investigation, and - at least in some cases - additional authentication secrets.

Using the SSO system does not require trust towards third parties, as opposed to systems based on an authentication proxy or similar architecture. The authentication secret is only handled by user and service, with the central authentication secret remaining on the user side – more specifically, on the token - at all times. The system offers an alternative to hash functions for the purpose of generating passwords on the fly. In addition to the capabilities of hash function based systems, the presented implementation makes use of the strength of smart card based two factor authentication. It also meets the technical requirements outlined in section 2.1, offering a mobile and interoperable dynamic authentication infrastructure built on legacy systems.

As the user can employ the solution for password management, we estimate that the perceived usefulness should be quite high. This in turn might ameliorate the acceptance of electronic signatures [13] [18], leading to a wider usage of signature cards and readers and to a more secure, multi-factor authentication infrastructure.

5   Conclusion

In this paper, a possible solution for the password management challenge users face today was presented, using electronic signatures for password generation. An overview of the architectural components of such a system was provided, and security requirements and guarantees were investigated. A prototype implementation that uses a signature capable SIM card was presented. The underlying architecture may also be used with other signature cards, like electronic id-cards, that are being rolled out in several member states of the European Union. Integrating electronic signatures with password legacy systems would increase the number of transactions where signatures are used. Therefore, the technology acceptance of electronic signatures might also be increased.

References

1. Abadi, M., Bharat, K. and Marais, J. (1997) System and method for generating unique passwords, United States Patent 6141760.
2. Adams, A., Sasse, M. A. and Lunt, P. (1997) Making Passwords Secure and Usable, Proceedings of HCI on People and Computers XII, Bristol, UK, Springer, 1-19.

3. Ball, P. (2001) Hacktivism and Human Rights: Using Technology to Raise the Bar, Panel Discussion, DEF CON 9, Las Vegas, USA.

4. Brown, B. J. and Callis, K.(2004) Computer Password Choice and Personality Traits Among College Students, Southeast Missouri State University, Cape Girardeau, Missouri, USA.

5. De Cock, D., Wouters, K. und Preneel, B. (2004) Introduction to the Belgian EID Card, S. K. Katsikas, S. Gritzalis und J. Lopez (Eds.), Public Key Infrastructures, Berlin Heidelberg, Springer, 1-13.

6. Economides, N. (1996) The Economics of networks, International Journal of Industrial Organization, 14, 673-699.

7. Fraunhofer SIT (2006) Der PasswordSitter, White Paper.

8. Gabber, E., Gibbons, P., Matias, Y. and Mayer, A. (1997) How to Make Personalized Web Browsing Simple, Secure and Anonymous, Proceedings of the First International Conference on Financial Cryptography, Anguilla, British West Indies, Springer, 17-32.

9. Halderman, J. A., Waters, B. and Felten, E. W. (2005) A convenient method for securely managing passwords, WWW '05: Proceedings of the 14th international conference on World Wide Web, Chiba, Japan, ACM Press, 471-479.

10. Hvarre, J. (2004) Electronic signatures in Denmark: free for all citizens, e-Signature Law Journal, 1, 1, 12-17.

11. Ives, B., Walsh, K. and Schneider, H. (2004) The Domino Effect of Password Reuse, Communications of the ACM, 4, 47, 75-78.

12. Karp, A.H. (2003) Site-Specific Passwords, Technical Report, HP Laboratories Palo Alto.

13. Lopez, J., Opplinger, R. and Pernul, G. (2005) Why Have Public Key Infrastructures Failed So Far? Internet Research, 15, 5, 544 - 556.

14. RSA Security (2005) RSA Security Survey Reveals Multiple Passwords Creating Security Risks and End User Frustration: Press Release, http://www.rsasecurity.com/press_release.asp?doc_id=6095, September 27.

15. Rivest, R. L., Shamir, A. and Adleman, L. (1978) A Method for Obtaining Digital Signatures and Public Key Cryptosystems, Communications of the ACM, 21, 2, 120-126.

16. Ross, B., Jackson, C., Miyake, N., Boneh, D. and Mitchell, J. C. (2005) Stronger Password Authentication Using Browser Extensions, Proceedings of the 14th Usenix Security Symposium, Baltimore, Maryland.

17. Roßnagel, H., Zibuschka, J. (2007) Integrating Qualified Electronic Signatures with Password Legacy Systems, Digital Evidence Journal, 4, 1, 1-10.

18. Roßnagel, H. (2007) Mobile Qualifizierte Elektronische Signaturen: Analyse der Hemmnisfaktoren und Gestaltungsvorschläge zur Einführung, unpublished doctoral dissertation, Department of Business Administration and Economics, Johann Wolfgang Goethe University, Frankfurt am Main.

19. Savard, J. (1999) Keystream Base Conversion and Random Bit Unbiasing, A Cryptographic Compendium.

20. Secure Information Technology Center – Austria (2006) The Austrian Citizen Card, http://www.buergerkarte.at/index_en.html, February 28.

21. Weitzel, T. (2003) A Network ROI, Proceedings of the MISQ Academic Workshop on ICT standardization, ICIS 2003, Seattle WA, USA.